FROM MULTI TO BILATERALISM:

AN ASSUMPTION FOR THE NEW GLOBAL TRADE

CARLO BARBIERI

MASTER'S DISSERTATION PRESENTED AS A PARTIAL REQUIREMENT FOR OBTAINING THE TITLE OF *MASTER OF SCIENCE IN LEGAL STUDIES* UNDER THE GUIDANCE OF PROF. DR. DOUGLAS DE CASTRO.

Publisher: Ambra University Press
First edition: December 13, 2021 (Revision 1.0a)

Author: Carlo Barbieri Filho
Title: From Multilateralism to Bilateralism: An assumption for the new Global Trade
Cover design: Jhonny Santos
Book design: Ambra University Press
Proofreading: Ambra University Press
E-book format: EPUB
Print format: Paperback- 6 x 9 inch

Library of Congress Control Number: 2021952397
ISBN: 978-1-952514-26-5 (Print - Paperback)
ISBN: 978-1-952514-27-2 (e-book – EPUB)

Ambra is a trademark of Ambra Education, Inc. registered in the U.S. Patent and Trademark Office.
Ambra University Press is a division of Ambra Education, Inc.
Orlando, FL, USA
https://press.ambra.education/ • https://www.ambra.education/

Editora: Ambra University Press
Primeira edição: 13 de dezembro de 2021 (Revisão 1.0a)

Autor: Carlo Barbieri Filho.
Título: From Multilateralism to Bilateralism: An assumption for the new Global Trade
Design da capa: Jhonny Santos
Projeto gráfico: Ambra University Press
Revisão: Ambra University Press
Formato e-book: EPUB
Formato impresso: Capa mole - 6 x 9 polegadas

Número de Controle da Library of Congress: 2021952397
ISBN: 978-1-952514-26-5 (Impresso – capa mole)
ISBN: 978-1-952514-27-2 (e-book – EPUB)

Ambra é uma marca da Ambra Education, Inc. registrada no U.S. Patent and Trademark Office.
Ambra University Press é uma divisão da Ambra Education, Inc.
Orlando, FL, EUA
https://press.ambra.education/ • https://www.ambra.education/

I dedicate this research to my family.

SUMÁRIO

PREFACE

The term globalization is the typical concept that is operationalized according to the convenience of those who want to use the term.

Although the roots of globalization can be disputed, some events may indicate that its process did not start with the great European navigations. The ancient Silk Road connected China with other countries 1-century bC. The prophet Mohammed was a great merchant in the Middle East, doing business in several countries in the Middle East.[1]

The end of World War II opened the doors to a new world economic order that recognized, through the Bretton Woods Institutions, the rise of the United States and the former USSR as great world powers, marking the decline of European power (which still had to deal with revolutionary waves in colonies dominated by European countries). The two pillars of Bretton Woods, finance and international trade, needed to be promoted worldwide as a form of peacekeeping. Thus, the International Monetary Fund, the World Bank, the General Agreement on Tariffs and Trade (GATT), and the World Trade Organization were charged with facilitating and harmonizing the rules that would sustain globalization.

The term begins to be used more frequently in the early 1990s as a natural response to the collapse of the former USSR and its satellite states, pointing to an inevitable scenario that Francis Fukuyama theorizes as "The End of

---

1   https://www.weforum.org/agenda/2019/01/how-globalization-4-0-fits-into-the-history-of-globalization/. Last access: Nov 9, 2021.

History",[2] that is, the prevalence of liberalism over socialism as a form of political and economic organization.

In this way, globalization became the buzzword of the following decades, constituting a kind of process in which one could not fight against it, under the penalty of swimming against the tide. In its triumphant beginnings, globalization had a dimension associated with it: the world economy. Despite being a dimension of great importance, the complexities that arise in the international system are beginning to challenge the prevalence of the economic dimension, bringing new challenges that need to be addressed.

The military and cultural dimensions brought about by the 9/11 attacks could not be ignored. It is on this occasion that another thesis that emerges at the end of the Cold War gains new traction in political and academic debates: Samuel Huntington's The Clash of Civilizations,[3] which puts, in short, the displacement of conflicts between states to conflicts between existing civilizations in the world. Issues related to international security and armed conflicts become part of the tangle of phenomena that make up a more complete picture of globalization. But not the only one!

---

2   https://www.jstor.org/stable/24027184?Search=yes&resultItemClick=true&searchText=francis%20fukuyama%20end%20of%20history&searchUri=%2Faction%2FdoBasicSearch%3FQuery%3Dfrancis%2Bfukuyama%2Bend%2Bof%2Bhistory%26so%3Drel&ab_segments=0%2Fbasic_search_gsv2%2Fcontrol&refreqid=fastly-default%3Ad216b1a27abf11e6618acb082ed9e25e. Last access: Nov 8, 2021.

3   https://www.jstor.org/stable/20045621?Search=yes&resultItemClick=true&searchText=clash%20of%20civilization&searchUri=%2Faction%2FdoBasicSearch%3FQuery%3Dclash%2Bof%2Bcivilization%26acc%3Doff%26wc%3Don%26fc%3Doff%26group%3Dnone%26refreqid%3Dsearch%253A48e15b19e2bdbdebd8f6e764f44f30b1%26so%3Drel&ab_segments=0%2Fbasic_search_gsv2%2Fcontrol&refreqid=fastly-default%3Aebfe9be2f58a122c71865f94101a6f30. Last access: Nov 8, 2021.

Climate change and the loss of biodiversity brought to the concept of globalization an environmental dimension that could no longer be relegated, being considered as existential threats to humanity. In this context, what will be, for example, the economic and social consequences of the announcement and the start of actions by China to reduce its carbon emissions to zero?

To continue in the environmental dimension, the response of the United States concerning the environmental goals and commitments of China, its biggest rival on the international scene today, translates into Build Back Better, a program that aims to make the US economy greener to join the "wave" of environmental globalization. As well placed by Foreign Affairs:

> *Without such preparations, the energy transition may add to the unfortunate and painful history of regionalized joblessness. It could fuel more misery, broken families, and addiction. Regional economic divides have intensified political polarization in the United States and provided fertile ground for populists. If the federal government is serious about decarbonizing the U.S. economy, then it must also get serious about helping people who will lose their jobs in the process.*[4]

As can be seen, the implications of globalization go far beyond the economic dimension and involve a myriad of aspects, connections, effects, vulnerabilities, impacts social and perceptions, to name a few, that prevent

---

4   https://www.foreignaffairs.com/articles/united-states/2021-11-08/china-shocks-lessons-green-economy?utm_medium=newsletters&utm_source=fatoday&utm_campaign=The%20China%20Shock%E2%80%99s%20Lessons%20for%20the%20Green%20Economy&utm_content=20211108&utm_term=FA%20Today%20-%20112017. Last access: Nov 10, 2021.

its conceptualization from being universal and monolithic, as its most ardent defenders intended in the early 1990s.

The ontology and epistemology of globalization have undergone major changes in recent decades to the point of preventing a more precise identification and the scope of its implications in the most diverse areas and spheres of the national and international social strata. The perception of globalization can be summarized in the analogy of the car at high speed on the highway, whose rear-view mirror warns in a recorded message "objects may look smaller than they appear", that is, we have already abandoned a lot, but be careful with the approaching, while the windshield reminds us to look ahead, but it's dirty because the wiper is faulty.

The great merit of this work is to outline a new vision for economic globalization, which in my view, in its formula, incorporates other dimensions of globalization (existing and others that are yet to come). It does precisely by pointing to a new epistemology for globalization that is counterintuitive if we take into account its "global" nature: the abandonment of universal formulas and practices in favor of regional and sectoral approaches that can make more sense and more efficiently managed.

The work drives the debate in the sense of pointing out the weaknesses and obstacles that the Bretton Woods Institutions in the pillar of international trade, GATT and the WTO, face in recent decades, especially considering the blocking of the Doha Round and the rise of nationalist governments that adopt more protectionist postures, emptying the multilateral system of international trade. This is without counting the important environmental implications that are brought into focus in the regulation of international trade and finance.

On the other hand, these movements encourage countries to sign international agreements on a reduced spectrum in terms of the number of participants and specific content, which in this book sheds more light on bilateral investment treaties (BIT).

According to the Investment Policy Hub of the United Nations Conference on Trade and Development, since 1957, UN member countries have signed

2,826 BITs, of which 2,258 are in force, that is, a large volume of international agreements between two countries to couple their national interests more quickly and specialized.[5] Furthermore, this became a strategy of developing countries as a way to ease the economic interdependence of some countries, especially the United States, which since then has been the great guarantor of the world economic order due to 1) being the controller of decisions in the IMF and World Bank because of the voting system and 2) by emptying multilateral international trade negotiations.

Thus, the question is: is the fragmentation observed empirically in the proliferation of BITs a sign that globalization, as a process, is losing traction? The answer is found in the present work, which points towards a transformation of globalization as an all-embracing phenomenon, towards a more palpable and operational phenomenon that can measure the implications for the various facets of globalization.

---

5   https://investmentpolicy.unctad.org/international-investment-agreements. Last access: Nov 10, 2021.

INTRODUCTION

At the end of the twentieth century, who could have foreshadowed a world outside of the brand new, widespread context of globalization? Could a " formula " that permeated the entire social construction of countries and their relations over the past three decades change its logic?

A one-off 2009 study by researcher Luiz Carlos Delorme Prado[1], focused on the applicable conceptual understanding of the term globalization . The author was unable to specify the exact period and the origin of the expression. However, mentioned the term in works published since the mid-1980s. Some works[2], according to him, marks the emergence of the concept.

> *"The concept of globalization began to be used since the mid-1980s, replacing concepts such as internationalization and transnationalization. Originally, this idea was supported by sectors that advocated the greater participation of developing countries, in particular the Latin American and Asian NICs (New Industrialized Countries) in an internationally managed economy. (Prado, 2009, p.01)"*

---

[1]   Professor at the Institute of Economics at UFRJ, Ph.D in Economics from the University of London.

[2]   Harvey's book, 1989, a highly influential work published in the 1980s that deals with the theme of Globalization. Another work is the book by Gilpin, 1987, chapter 9 is dedicated to "The transformation of the Global Political Economy". There is also the work of Gill & Law who published in 1989, the book entitled "The Global Political Economy".

According to Prado (2009, p.3), only in the late 1980s and early 1990s the term globalization began to be used, particularly, in two senses: " one positive, describing the process of integration of the world economy; and a normative, describing a development strategy based on rapid integration with the world economy". That was the starting point of the research by the static conceptual definition of globalization, studies that opened numerous possible interpretations on the subject.

"One can, however, perceive four basic lines of interpretation of the phenomenon: (i) - globalization as a historical time; (ii) - globalization as a sociological phenomenon of space and time compression; (iii) globalization as hegemony of liberal values; (iv) globalization as a socioeconomic phenomenon. An example of the first approach is the position of the influential journalist Ignacio Ramonet, who defines Globalization as the main characteristic of the historical cycle we entered, after the fall of the Berlin Wall (1989) and the disappearance of the Soviet Union (1991). (Prado, 2009, p. 02)"

These multiple interpretations will lead to different paths of analysis. This analysis will tie its work to the idea of globalization as compression of space and time, broadcasted by sociologists David Harvey (1989) and Anthony Giddens (1990 - 1999). The concept was elevated to the economic prism by Agnew & Corbridge (1995, p.217),

> "The organization of the space defines relationships, not only between activities, things and concepts, but also between people. The organization of the space defines social relations. The freedom of capital to move around the world (...). Therefore, this compression of space and time, made possible by technological changes in the contemporary world, would give increasing power to globalized capital (...)."

Although, as noted, there isn't an academic accepted and defined concept, one must understand that the logic of globalization was born long ago. The Silk Road, for example, was already testing the model of trade between countries. The great navigations started the global exchange of products, values, cultures - a process that was expanded between the 15th and 17th centuries, when there was a growing search for exploring new territories and doing trade. This will be considered the cradle of international relations between countries.

It will be understood by this research, that the globalization is not a European phenomenon, but a process that evolves from the expansion of world trade to the East, which in return has established a process of globalization with Chinese characteristics. At the beginning of the 20th century, political, economic, cultural and technological conditions started to be more favorable to globalization. After World War II, the phenomenon began to gain strength in the western capitalist world, led by the United States with the participation of Europe and Japan. The world was practically divided into two poles: the liberal-capitalist world and the socialist-communist world. led by Russia.

The assumption that will be defended in this work is that the analysis is in some ways positive and negative of globalization throughout its evolution, it is possible to notice anomalies in multilateralism of trade and new global tendency form bilateral agreements - which will contemplate more advantageously the interests of countries linked to that particular trade relationship.

To move forward, however, a punctual definition of the historical context and the concept of multilateralism will be needed.

> "(...) the understanding of multilateralism as a dynamic of international relations that has been marking and changing the nature of the interaction between States and their people. Widespread in the Cold War, this is already an institutionalized phenomenon and less and less circumvented by state legislators. However, the United Nations system is an example that demonstrates the relationship between "power

politics" and multilateralism, in a game that contributes both
to reinforce and to diminish the role of multilateral bodies.
(Fernandes & Simão, 2019, p.09)"

The authors consider the phenomenon of multilateralism to be a form of cooperation for collective decision-making. And that, although the concept emerged after the Industrial Revolution of the 19th century, "in the form of multilateral agreements that aimed at responding to the political, social and economic transformations of the time, we consider that it only becomes a systemic practice later" (Fernandes & Simão , 2019, p.20) .

This systemic practice key to the conceptual and theoretical gear on which this work is concerned. The understanding of multilateralism and its practice over the years, will help to understand the moment that marks its eventual end in postmodern society.

"(...) the multilateral option was able to become cheaper,
more utilitarian and, at the same time, able to manage more
effectively everything that the government could not only
solve, but risk compromising. In this respect, multilateralism
gains its post-modernity outlines. (Badie, 2007, p.231)"

This scenario, which has been promising for global multilateralism, has shown signs of profound change. What we want to analyze in this work is that many countries are surrendering to a possible new global business structure returning to bilateralism over multilateralism. The United States for example, since the Barak Obama administration and even more recent and evident during the current Donald Trump administration, clearly demonstrates that it is changing the route in this context.

There are indications that with the start of trade war with China, the US began to further guide its interests through bilateral agreements with other countries of the world - a practice that comparatively analyze this work. Thus, it will be presented the following scenario, the problem, the object of research and methodology that is intended to apply in the study.

Chapter 2 of this paper, will address an analysis of globalization and its nuances. It will mention concepts of financial globalization, production, and will present some positive and negative aspects of the phenomenon.

In chapter 3, this research will deal with precisely the trade blocs and bring an introduction to multilateralism. Mentioning the current regulation of trade, commercial blocks and a possible introduction to multilateralism, displaying the anomalies of this concept, new ways to globalization, and finally, a relation paradox between China and the US, Brexit and arrive at the theoretical assumption of bilateral agreements - a path to the logic of bilateralism. Also addressing the legal aspects of the controversy relations of the WTO agreements.

In Chapter 4, this research will apply this new scenario and case study. A map of the multi to bilateralism will be presented. Bringing the analysis of background conditions, the possible new aspects of globalization and end Geo policy. Comparing the trade war between China and the US, as a parameter for a global trade change.

Possible micro causes for the path from multi to bilateralism will be presented and, finally, the trade agreements signed by the American governments over the past 20 years will be studied. In chapter 5, the final considerations of this work will be presented. And in the Chapter 6, the references of which this research was based.

SCENARIO

As presents the brief introduction, the following parameters will be presented that guide us in this study. From the formatting of the scenario to the methodological definition

to be followed.

All states, people, and individuals on the planet have gradually become part of a global world in the last two decades of the twentieth century. However, over the years, since the establishment of the World Trade Organization - WTO, and in the face of a changing world scenario, the dynamics of the globalization process have undergone significant changes, which have not been translated into new rules. This transformation process has caused countries to restructure regulations for free trade agreements or bilateral agreements, which may propel the WTO to the margins and drive more fragmented and less group-based government structures.

From one point it started to become increasingly clear that there was a depletion of processes of globalization because the rules designed to manage it did not protect parties fairly. Both developing and developed countries are frustrated by the slow pace of multilateral trade and integration in negotiations, which has resulted in an unprecedented parallel agreement without growth, according to data released by Applied Research Institute of Brazil - IPEA.

Since the world's first bilateral investment promotion and reciprocal protection agreement, signed by Germany and Pakistan in 1959, the bilateral investment promotion and protection agreements, or BITs, of the English Bilateral Investment Treaty, have increased, especially in recent years. Currently, there are thousands of bilateral investment agreements in force, involving most countries in the world.

The process of signing bilateral investment treaties was born mainly as a response by investors from developed countries to the nationalization movements that took place in developing countries and to the appeals of these countries ensured by the multilateral instrument - the Charter of Social Economic Rights and Duties of States (Resolution United Nations No. 3281 1974).

In this new scenario, it is necessary to analyze the phenomenon of transition from multilateralism in trade relations to new ways of conducting economic and international policies in the world economic aspects. It is possible that the new globalization is being structured by the way bilateral agreements have been made today.

QUESTION

The hypothesis to be studied brings an analysis of the notable decrease in multilateral meetings at the WTO, which leads to the assertion that there is a transformation of the globalization process, and in parallel, there is a significant increase in bilateral agreements to the detriment of multilateral agreements, until then in the majority.

The case study will serve as a parameter for the hypothesis raised and should evaluate the trend of the United States as a likely promoter of the new economic world order based on bilateral agreements and, in this sense, bring to light the most recent agreements signed by that country in this bipolar format, as well as elucidating its influence in diminishing the power of international commerce, military and health organizations.

In this way, the context that points to 1) the movement of decreasing meetings at the WTO will be considered; 2) the increase in the conclusion of bilateral agreements; 3) the new world economic order that has been establishing and changing the globalization process initiated by multilateral treaties; and 4) the influence of this change on the world political and commercial scenario, asking, based on this research, what will be the world economic future and its trade relations.

Answering these questions is important when choosing a research method that has an exploratory and analytical character.

PURPOSE OF THE RESEARCH

Based on the context presented above, in the preliminary review of the literature and the existing data on the topic, we will seek to analyze the increase in the conclusion of bilateral agreements observed over the past eight years in the United States and will seek to understand whether the conclusion of these agreements depletes the importance of the WTO - redirecting global foreign trade from multilateral to bilateral logic. The trade agreements signed by the United States during President Barack Obama's final four years in office and President Donald Trump's first term will be examined.

OBJECTIVES

The general objective that is sought is to understand whether there has been an increase in the signing of trade agreements under the logic of bilateralism in the United States in the last eight years. As specific objectives of this research, the following points are listed:

- search for a possible relationship between the increase in the number of bilateral agreements in the USA and the rupture in WTO hegemony;

- infer concepts inherent to this new commercial scenario;

- present analyzes of the commercial agreements entered into and;

- describe the importance of this new paradigm for world foreign trade.

METHODOLOGY

To reach the objective, it will be necessary to respond to the research hypothesis that leads to the analysis of points of resistance, since in the current format - even with the tendency towards bilateral agreements, this change should break with the whole structure that created globalization: the capitalist groups, China, a substantial part of the European Union (currently managed by countries that have a particular interest in globalization - France and Germany) and some segments of the world economy.

Does this process, contrary to the expectations of everyone who has gained from globalization, have a chance of success? Or will there be an attempt by these segments, which have benefited, to create a new way in which globalization is maintained in the previous terms, favoring in part to the view of this new market reality?

Therefore there is a hypothesis: the increase in bilateral agreements has led to the emptying of meetings at the WTO, which indicates a significant ontological change in the globalization process.

Therefore, the methodology that will be applied in this research is based on descriptive and analytical research with the approach anchored in Pragmatic Semiotics, which contemplates not only the analysis of the text, but encompasses possible inferences regarding the context, not being restricted to observance only. the agreements concluded between the USA and other countries, but also to the related context of this possible increase in bilateral agreements with an "emptying" of WTO power. It will also be valid to discuss the digressive strategies that involve the context.

The qualitative nature of the methodology that will be adopted in the work is linked to the purpose of the research in promoting a microanalysis of the causal process to capture the dynamic interactions existing in the phenomenon, which is to say that the internal pressures of the capitalist elites may be bringing about a transformation of the globalization process and the consequent increase in bilateralism in the conclusion of trade agreements between countries. The objective is to verify which phenomena may have led to the emptying of multilateralism.

To achieve this objective in the research, the techniques of process tracing (PT) and analysis of the main commercial agreements signed by the United States in the last 20 years will be adopted. "PT in Social Sciences is the basic type of scientific research that has an exploratory and analytical character in the sense of better understanding multi-causal phenomena and whose interactions are difficult to capture." (Brady & Collier, 2010, p.4)

> *"This technique involves the careful observation of the phenomenon and the examination of evidence in a study of cases that may contribute to confirm or not the research hypothesis, thus solving methodological difficulties that have arisen in quantitative research." (Bennett, 2005, p.26)*[3]

With this technique, the identification of conditions minimally sufficient to measure the inferred contribution in the research hypothesis will be sought and if there was no contribution, what are the relevant factors for its non-occurrence, in addition to detecting other factors or variables that may be important for the study. (Beach & Pedersen, 2013, p.170)

It is intended to apply the PT in the main US trade agreements based on the following categories of analysis. Below are the applications of the analysis categories:

1. **nature of the agreement:** in this category, it will be identified whether the agreement was supported by multilateralist or bilateralism logic;

2. **date and repercussions:** this subcategory will analyze the date of the agreement and its possible repercussions in the political and economic spheres;

3. **Rupture of the Multilateral logic:** this topic will be investigated if there was a break in the American multilateral agreements, what they meant before

---

3   The PT manages to: 1) establish the causal direction unequivocally; 2) to remove the influence of hidden variables in the model; and / or 3) to detect the existence of a spuriousness relationship between the study variables.

in terms of foreign trade, pointing out if they were positive or negative for the American economy.

4. Adoption of the Bilateralism logic: this topic will investigate any new bilateral agreements signed by the governments and how much this represents in terms of commercial advantage and rebalancing of American world trade

5. General conclusion: this topic will be sought to infer which are the perspectives within these trend graphs that they will be able to obtain for the new world economic scenario, always taking into account the American case.

George and Bennett (2004, p.19) state that the selection of cases must be part of the researcher's strategy according to his objectives and it must meet two basic requirements, namely, 1) the cases must be relevant to the research objective; and 2) they must be selected to maintain the control demanded by the research question.

To gain analytically from the case study, this research must still use two or more cases and recognize the existence of a strong positive association between the study variables, thus selecting cases where the values of these variables are present. (Gerring & Seawright , 2008, p.38).

Thus, the selection of cases will follow the typical case modality, whose objective is to obtain representative cases of a population of potential cases to test the research hypothesis (Gerring & Seawright, 2008).

As a result of the methodological considerations on the selection of cases and the object of the research, the object focus will be centered on the commercial agreements signed in the United States during the last four years of ex-President Barack Obama's term and the four years of current President Donald Trump's term.

The choice of cases is justified as being both representative for the analysis of the phenomenon of breaking the multilateral agreements in which the United States was involved at that time. It is also necessary to assess the evolution of events in the economic scenario at the end of the Obama era and the beginning of the Trump era in order to define the initial moment of this transformation.

In the course of the investigation, other possible implications will be identified vis-à-vis the formulated research hypothesis.

As the main scientific contribution, the present project will produce original empirical data on the possibilities and reasons for existing, from two points of view: reduction of multilateral agreements and increase of bilateral agreements, a worldwide trend today.

The analysis of hypotheses and possibilities will bring some answers about this new world trend that is worth studying, because it will not die either by success or failure. If there is a change in American policy, globalization may gain space again and these concepts that we are going to rise will have more strength, but it will not cause the ideas of bilateral agreements to cease to exist. Therefore, this study can contribute positively to the future regardless of the world scenario to be formed after the American election of 2020.

The expected results will make it possible to expand the knowledge of the way of which trade agreements are concluded and how it can change the course of globalization. Added to this result is the development of a future broader research agenda with regard to the world economic scenario.

POST-GLOBALIZATION: A WORLD IN TRANSFORMATION

As stated, globalization is the scenario on which this research is focused. A premise that will guide to identify which future movement should be expected in the global context of foreign trade and international legislation. It will be anchored in a definition that understands globalization as a socioeconomic phenomenon with real impacts on political, economic and legal contexts.

"The idea of Globalization as a socioeconomic phenomenon was supported by authors such as Reinaldo Gonçalves (1999) who argued that globalization can be defined as the interaction of three distinct processes, which have occurred over the past 20 years, and which affect the financial dimensions, commercial and technological of international economic relations. (Gonçalves, 1999. p.20)"

This assumption added to the conclusion of Prado (2009, p.5) will guarantee the distinction of the already consolidated worlds of globalization to later present a possible resizing of the current logic that governs this phenomenon - multilateralism.

"We define Globalization as the process of integrating domestic markets, in the process of forming an integrated world market (...). In this sense, the phenomenon of Globalization can be divided into three processes, which, are deeply interconnected through: commercial globalization, financial globalization and productive globalization. (Prado, 2009, p. 04)"

Globalization has been accepted as one of the most used definitions to describe the totality of the capitalist system and its dominance in the world. In reality, globalization is understood as the total or partial integration between different regions of the world to promote relevant issues globally.

The concept that we will present, considers the phenomenon as a process that is constantly changing, evolving.

For Stiglitz (2002, p.37), globalization has two controversial faces: on one hand, knowledge reached populations through this phenomenon, which may have helped international trade and fostered the growth of many countries. On the other hand, the phenomenon has generated inequalities with economic advantages for some countries and increased levels of poverty for others.

Prado (2009, p.14) still defends "the popular use of the concept of globalization as an expression of an economic change produced by the dynamics of technological innovations, being both an inevitable and desirable phenomenon, it is imprecise, but fulfills its role of legitimizing a certain interpretation of the world".

To understand the dynamics of the globalization process, the three dimensions of the phenomenon will be presented, considered by Prado (2009): commercial, financial and productive.

COMMERCIAL GLOBALIZATION

Commercial globalization is understood as the integration of markets through international trade. It is measured from the average annual growth rate of trade worldwide. Commercial globalization materializes when the average annual growth rate becomes higher than the world GDP. When the phenomenon only occurs at the regional level, it is referred to as economic integration.

Commercial globalization is not a new phenomenon. The first occurrence was dated in the 1930s when the first moment of expansion of globalization occurred.

With the end of World War II, the growth of international trade encouraged, mainly by the USA, spurred the search for specific rules to facilitate multilateral agreements between countries. GATT, created after the Havana Conference in 1947, brought rules to regulate trade relations (exchanges and sales) at the international level.

"GATT was an important step for international trade, adopting principles that today are the basis of the main rules of the World Trade Organization, the WTO. After its foundation, the WTO started to play an important role in the regulation of world trade, having as one of its main objectives the search for the development of the so-called countries of the economic "south", the underdeveloped countries. (Prado, 2009, p 29)"

The WTO then emerged, already with a clear track record in resolving disputes between signatory countries. As a result, as Prado points out, commercial globalization is the easiest to quantify. (2009, p.25).

"Trade globalization is the most easily measurable and its discussion is not particularly controversial: if the growth of world trade occurs at an average annual growth rate higher than that of world GDP, we can say that there is trade globalization".

FINANCIAL GLOBALIZATION

Another concept that is interesting in the scope of this research is financial globalization. According to Plihon (2007, p.83), financial globalization can be defined as a process of interconnection of capital markets at national levels (markets for loans and financing, public and private securities, monetary, foreign exchange, etc.) and leading to the emergence of a unified global money market.

The growth of international flows and the deregulation of financial services internationally have been accompanied by frequent crises, arising from the end of the Bretton-Woods system, the system negotiated to reorganize international economic relations after World War II, in order to avoid another major monetary instability. in attempts to recreate the gold standard. The assumptions guaranteed that: the dollar would be considered the reference currency of the system; fixed exchange rates would regulate the regime of other currencies; capital account with controlled speculative movements; the new monetary system would be supervised and operated by the IMF.

In the years of 1948 and 1971, the Bretton-Woods foundation, together with Keynesian policies, helped the USA and Western European countries. However, it faced a challenge, as it was not feasible to combine capital freedom and fixed exchange rates with an autonomous monetary policy aimed at domestic purposes. Thus,

"Financial globalization is the process of integrating local financial markets - such as the markets for loans and financing, government and private securities, monetary, foreign exchange, insurance, etc. international markets. In the end, national markets would operate only as a local expression of a large global financial market. Therefore, this phenomenon is not only about the growth of financial transactions abroad, but also about the integration of national financial markets in the formation of an international financial market. (Prado, 2009, p. 14)"

The standard of financial globalization started to be questioned for the regulation of the world economy. There was then a consensus for an international financial reform to take place to realign the globalization of markets.

The beginning of the 21st century brings to light the need for a "new Bretton Woods", a new exchange rate policy regime.

Still, according to Prado (2009, p.25), the financial dimension is the most important aspect of globalization. Since 1970, there has been a growth in financial transactions between countries. Two main characteristics are noted: the growth of savings mobility and the internationalization of financial services.

Financial globalization is an important tool for mediation and analysis of the financing levels of deficits in transactions in the world economy.

Rebel Technology and Banking Correspondence (2018) conceptualizes the term financial globalization as the integration of national and international financial systems and the increase of competition in the capital market and of what may interfere in the purchase and sale of shares.

We can consider that financial globalization is the interconnection of international financial markets and has fostered the global financial market. Which means that situations that happen anywhere in the world can affect a foreign company locally.

We will consider that the breakdown of markets, the deregulation of economic activity and the reduction of intermediaries are the main characteristics of financial globalization.

The concept, which appeared in the USA in the 1980s, promoted a great integration of world economic relations. Every time we think about the stock market, the foreign exchange market, the commodities market, the raw materials market, we are thinking about financial globalization.

In the purchase and sale of shares, raw materials, commodities or currency exchange, globalization is already happening within the economic-financial scenario and these markets are not affected only by the actions taken by those who participate in them. In the case of buying and selling commodities for example, crop losses due to bad weather, an accident or a health crisis in a given country, as examples, can cause price changes in the global financial market.

PRODUCTIVE GLOBALIZATION

Prado (2009, p.28) describes productive globalization as an international integration of the production chain. A macro system that integrates local companies, benefiting them with competitive advantages, use of technology and techniques. Companies that take advantage of oligopolies concentrated due to protectionist barriers, oligopolies differentiated by the strength of their brands, and increasing returns to scale,

"The productive dimension of globalization is one of its most complex and difficult aspects to deal with. In our definition, we call productive globalization the process of integrating domestic productive structures into an international productive structure. (Prado, 2009, p.7)."

International direct investment causes the process of productive globalization. The internationalization of market structures and global business competition are among the main factors observed in this phenomenon.

Transnational companies gain space and reflect their competitive advantages in international trade. The revolution in the media fueled the growth of commercial globalization through the development of technological conditions for greater international production integration.

ET′s (Modern Transnational Companies), gain greater projection and strength in the United States after the Second World War. The projection of American political and economic power and government support made the operations of companies abroad less risky and created a favorable environment in the host countries (Huntington, 1975, p.103).

"Japanese companies contributed to alter global competition, when from the 1980s they started to occupy market portions previously dominated by Western companies. This market share was possible because exports of final products did not come only from Japan, but from various production bases in East Asia, benefiting from the strong integration of the productive structure in that region. The product started to be identified no longer by the country in which it was produced, but by its quality through the brand. (PRADO, 2009 p. 09)".

The reaction of companies to the challenges of the international economy is what we call global competition.

The global market started to reorganize itself based on this new context. And this understanding assures us of the scenario that we are trying to outline in this work. A new standard form of global investment has emerged from the need for companies to occupy positions in large markets. Companies have become global players in this context.

"Productive globalization is one of the most important dimensions of the globalization phenomenon. Global companies are not stateless, since every company is connected to a specific country or set of countries, where its headquarters is located and where its political decision-making nucleus is located. From this nucleus, they negotiate with governments to project their strategic interests. (Prado, 2009, p. 10)."

The rise in taxes in transnational corporations' host countries resulted in them establishing their headquarters, for legal reasons, in countries that offered them better tax conditions or even exemption, allowing them to truly become independent of their original countries.

In this way, countries like the USA lost revenue, as their large companies immigrated to what would be called tax havens, in addition to the loss of jobs, as competition with developing countries, particularly Asian ones, offered excessively cheap labor, with unskilled workers. There was no social security, and the work was almost slave-like.

In this context, the need arises for the creation of international bodies and regulatory bodies for the economic and commercial discrepancies that have emerged. The WTO is the greatest example of this.

WTO: LEGAL REGULATION OF TRADE RELATIONS

In 1995, the origin of the World Trade Organization (WTO) emerged. A reworking of the General Agreement on Tariffs and Trade (GATT), signed in

1947. GATT pushed the rules of the multilateral trade system between 1948 and 1994.

A total of eight trade negotiations were mediated by GATT. The eighth negotiation, known as the Uruguay Round, culminated in the creation of the WTO and a new set of multilateral agreements that formed the normative body of the new Organization, which has since acted as the main body to manage the multilateral trading system.

According to its official page, the WTO "The organization aims to establish a common institutional framework to regulate trade relations between the different Members that comprise it, to establish a mechanism for the peaceful settlement of trade disputes, based on the trade agreements currently in force, and create an environment that allows for the negotiation of new trade agreements between Members. Currently, the WTO has 164 Members, with Brazil being one of the founding Members".

Figure 1 - World map with signs of all WTO member countries

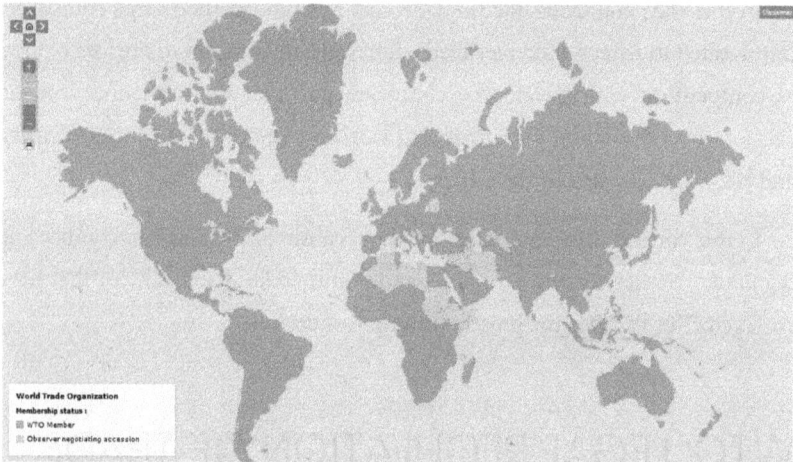

Source: WTO (2020).

International trade rules, according to the WTO, must be based on the principles of international trade law, which serve as a guide for many commercial decisions. The WTO has absorbed the principles that guide multilateral trade regulation from the GATT, the most notable of which are:

- Most-favored-nation principle: the WTO member must also offer assignment, privilege or benefit to all its trading partners, without differentiation. This principle aims to prevent privileges between countries. The exception occurs when privileged countries form an economic bloc;

- Principle of national treatment: when an imported service or product enters the territory of the importing member and ally must receive the same treatment as a similar the product or service provided;

- Principle of consolidation of commitments: the WTO member must offer other members treatment as favorable as provided in his list of its commitments;

- Principle of transparency: in order to be made clear to all involved, members must publicize all general decisions on international trade, regulations and laws.

The WTO is composed of several bodies, each with its own role. To date, eleven WTO Ministerial Conferences have been held, namely: Singapore (1996), Geneva (1998), Seattle (1999), Doha (2001), Cancun (2003), Hong Kong (2005), Geneva (2009 and 2011), Bali (2013), Nairobi (2015) and Buenos Aires (2017).

The Doha Round, launched at the Doha Ministerial Conference, was the first round of negotiations held at the WTO level and negotiations are ongoing. Tariffs, agriculture, services, trade facilitation, dispute settlement, and guidelines or "laws" were among the topics on the agenda for the Doha round.

Some authors, such as Bohnenberger and Weinhardt (2017, p.97), point out that the Doha Round negotiations, which have been going on for almost two decades, have not generated much results, meanwhile the need to write new rules that capture the changing nature of global trade rises. This scenario has been encouraging the filling of regulatory gaps arising from free trade agreements, whether regional or bilateral, a fact that leaves the WTO gradually more at the margin, generating more divided governance structures.

The structural and operational understanding of the WTO, allows us to conceive its relevance in the context of the problematic that is proposed for analysis. Later, it will be examined how and if this evolution contributes to the deepening of uncertainties about the future of the global trading system and its central institution, the World Trade Organization (WTO), resulting in increased fragmentation of global trade regulation and the emergence of anti-globalization sentiments that will define the trading system's future.

THE WTO SETTLEMENT DISPUTE SYSTEM

It is important to consider, in the perspective of this work, the dispute settlement system that was established within the scope of the WTO for the regulation of agreements in the multilateralist logic. Since the beginning of international relations, law has been used as a fundamental technique for achieving world peace and mediating agreements between countries.

"Law is an order of security, even though it cannot be said, as Kelsen points out in the 2nd edition of The Pure Theory of Law, that the state of law is necessarily a state of peace and that the securing of peace is an essential function of law, there is no doubt, in Kelsen's own words, that the development of law runs in this direction. (Lafer, 1996, p.03)."

Throughout history, law has been seen as a fundamental tool to enable peace between nations. This action takes place through the peaceful settlement of lawsuits.

"The settlement of disputes is, (...) an 'obligation of conduct' of the States, and it should be noted that it is not an obligation of results. This 'behavioral obligation' is seen as an indispensable integral part of bringing Friendly relations and cooperation among states in accordance with the Charter of the United Nations to recall the well-known 1970 UN General Assembly Resolution. (Lafer, 1996, p. 04)."

This legal assumption is necessary to understand the relevance of law in regulating the logic of multilateralism and its effectiveness in mediating conflicts and approving agreements between the blocs. Later, in the bilateral logic, this notion will show us that the Law continues to be a fundamental instrument in the composition of bilateral agreements, which may be due to presuppose the multilateralist logic, as will be investigated in this research.

"Art. 33, § - of the UN Charter lists these measures, and the 1982 Manila Declaration of the General Assembly on Peaceful Dispute Settlement (GA Resolution 37/10), which incorporates the 1970 Declaration on Friendly Relations, notes that the parties will choose peaceful means appropriate to the circumstances and nature of the dispute. As is well known, these techniques aimed at peaceful coexistence are negotiation, inquiry, mediation, conciliation, arbitration, judicial solution, which differ by the degree of control that the parties retain, or not, over the solution forwarding of a controversy. (Lafer, 1996, p.05)."

It is also necessary to consider that the legal structure of the WTO has been consolidated with a view to reducing friction and accommodating more general interests in the agreements concluded between countries. It is essential that the legislative bodies of each country approve the agreements concluded, and for this they are designed with a more simplistic and more direct perspective from the legal point of view. All in search of a quick and effective approval of its content. The same holds true in the bilateral logic of trade relations between countries. One way to achieve legislative approval of the agreements in the signatory countries.

The logic of the commercial blocs that we will present in the following chapter requires an understanding of the centrality of law in the regulation of commercial relations.

COMMERCIAL BLOCKS: AN INTRODUCTION TO MULTILATERALISM

In order to thoroughly investigate the concept of multilateralism, it is necessary to verify the origin and the reason for the formation of trade blocs between countries in the context of globalization. This positioning is critical in order to show that multilateralism docs not deny globalization, but rather emphasizes the most visible effect that has been studied thus far.

For this reason, the researchers Petri & Weber (2006)'s preliminary definition of commercial blocks, which focuses on observing the original context of commercial block formation at the level of the globalized society, becomes enthralling. A definition that will be accepted, as stated, to equate globalization and multilateralism as complementary to each other, rather than to put forward the concepts of globalization and multilateralism,

> *"It is believed that economic integration, through the formation of regional blocs, appears as a strategy for countries to protect themselves from the negative aspects of globalization. The expansion of an integrated economic space seems to be an alternative, not to stop the globalization process, but for countries to seek common order, respecting their own cultural, economic and social plurality, thus increasing the chances of reducing exclusion and projecting well-developed sectors. (Petri & Weber, 2006, p. 91)."*

Thus, the formation of economic blocs would aim to create conditions to foster and strengthen the economy of the globalized world. In all types of economic blocs, the idea is to reduce and / or eliminate import and export tariffs or taxes between member countries.

> *"In this context, the formation of blocks will take place, fueled by systems of forces that were once antagonistic: eliminating borders on the one hand, and preserving them on the other. (Petri & Weber, 2006, p. 91)."*

As a result, we will comprehend that the reduction of trade barriers is referred to as regionalism. (Bhagwati, 1999, p. 22).

Regionalism can also be thought of as a set of measures aimed at gradually eliminating discrimination between the economic units of different countries. (Balassa, 1980, p.1). The original purpose of economic blocs was to provide countries with a broad and multilevel (cultural, social, economic, and political) organization.

In this context, the formation of economic blocs can be viewed as an attempt to expand the consumer market, in which countries seek to make international trade relations more flexible. The agreements' goal is to establish treaties that will standardize tax actions among its members, such as tax exemptions or reductions on services and goods sold.

Economic blocs can provide for free movement of people between member countries of a given bloc and are not limited to customs tariff reductions or exemptions. They can be classified into the following categories based on their characteristics:

- **free trade zone:** agreement to cancel or reduce customs fees between the countries in the bloc. Example: the old North American Free Trade Agreement (NAFTA);

- **customs union:** reduces and eliminates the commercial tariffs between the countries of the bloc, as well as regulates, through the CET (Common External Tariff), trade with non-belonging nations, such as, for example, the Common Market of the South (MERCOSUR);

- **common market:** allows the free movement of services, capital and people within the bloc. Example: European Union (EU);

- **economic and monetary union:** countries practice the same development policy and a single currency. This is what is currently happening in the European Union.

The distribution of economic blocks across the world can be seen on the map in figure 2, below:

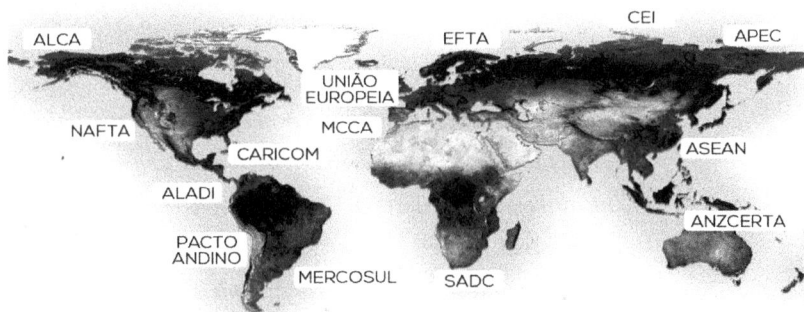

Figure 2 - Economic Blocs and intergovernmental organizations worldwide

Source: World of Education (2020).

The main economic blocs are:

- APEC - Economic Cooperation in Asia and the Pacific;

- ASEAN - Association of Southeast Asian Nations;

- CARICOM - Caribbean Common Market and Community;

- CEI - Community of Independent States;

- CAN - Comunidad Andina (Andean Pact until 1996);

- MCCA - Central American Common Market;

- MERCOSUR - Southern Common Market;

- NAFTA - North American Free Trade Agreement;

- SADC - Southern African Development Community;

- EU - European Union.

It is important to note, however, that some researchers argue that the bloc is ultimately a product of the National State, and particularly of the border preservationist vector.

> "*Seeking a greater or lesser integration among its members, notably economically, the bloc would be the way for countries to strengthen themselves together, avoiding facing international competition in isolation. Since, free-trade appears only in the discourse, because in practice protectionism has not disappeared. Others, however, see the formation of blocs as an escalation towards the abolition of borders, at least economic ones, constituting a regionalization of space that tends to become integrally global. (Petri & Weber, 2006, p. 92).*"

The investigation of the concept of multilateralism will be presented next, based on the scenario that has been addressed thus far. An analysis that will be crucial in this project in order to verify the concept's eventual defeat by a more bilateral logic.

The concept of multilateralism should be pursued based on the historical aspect very well consolidated by two other researchers, Sandra Fernandes and

Licínia Simão (2019). They present an in-depth look at the emergence of the logic of multilateralism that will also be mentioned in this work.

The authors present the outline of a multilateralism based world on the so-called European Concert, created in 1815, after the Napoleonic wars. In this period, the European powers decided to schedule regular meetings in times of peace, for the "good of Europe" (Fernandes & Simão, 2019, p.20),

> "Multilateral cooperation is, at first glance, a form of cooperation conducive to collective decision-making. Despite having arisen after the Industrial Revolution of the 19th century in the form of multilateral agreements, which aimed to respond to the political, social and economic transformations of the time, we consider that it only became a systemic practice afterwards. When American President Woodrow Wilson in 1918 spelled out the '14 points' that were to guide the terms of peace at the end of the first world war, multilateralism was an integral part of his view of the postwar international order. (Fernandes & Simão, 2019, p.20)."

This historical cut depicts the moment in world history when the ideal of multilateralism is realized. This scenario is extremely important because it is proposed in this paper to see if a new global logic is emerging that will presuppose the concept of multilateralism and its current dominance.

According to this premise, multilateralism is a subjective logic that hovers over global political and economic organization, coordinating, limiting, and obeying an irregular and non-standardized flow of agreements and decisions between block countries.

> "(...) to propose an understanding of 'multilateralism', as a dynamic of international relations that has marked

and changed the nature of the interaction between States and their people, in a very visible way since 1945. This is an institutionalized phenomenon, widely disseminated in the Cold War period, and less and less circumvented by state actors. However, the United Nations system is an example that demonstrates the relationship between "power politics" and multilateralism in a game that contributes both to reinforce and to diminish the role of multilateral bodies. (Fernandes & Simão, 2019, p. 09)."

This understanding allows us to infer the dynamics operated by multilateralism in the global context. A logic that interferes in the whole context of globalization in the world of politics, economics, and the sovereignty of countries and forces the construction and organization of a structure of international relations between countries based on diplomacy, a point that will be mentioned later.

"The phenomenon (multilateralism) is thus inserted in post-modernity as the multilateral option can become more economical, more utilitarian, and, at the same time, capable of managing more effectively and sharing everything that power not only cannot resolve but risks aggravating. In this respect, multilateralism gains its post-modernity outlines. (Badie, 2006, p. 231)."

It is also understood that multilateralism can be defined as the indiscriminate reduction of barriers to trade, understanding that the term "indiscriminate" is used in the sense that the reduction of barriers extends to all countries inserted in the world system of commerce (Bhagwati, 1999, p. 22).

ANOMALIES OF MULTILATERALISM AND THE NEW DIRECTIONS OF GLOBALIZATION

Some inconsistencies in the previously presented multilateralist model will be discussed below. A necessary cut in order to identify an eventual transition of logical models with implications for globalization governance.

In the late 1990s, waves of financial crises in emerging economies challenged the apologetics of a world without borders as an unsettling tsunami (Gama & Camargo, 2018). This moment is a milestone for what is considered the beginning of a break with the central logic of multilateralism until then.

It will be important to consider that numerous changes of power took place in the 1990s. These changes to the global power structures, which were felt, more particularly with the dismemberment of the Soviet Union in 1991, had an impact on the multilateral agenda and on expectations regarding management. governmental issues, as shown by researchers Fernandes & Simão (2019, p.27),

> *"The unipolar moment in the United States was predicted to be particularly visible in two central dimensions of the international agenda. On one hand, on security issues, where the complex emergencies of the 1990s challenged the UN and in other regional organizations to develop more effective mechanisms for conflict prevention, crisis management and humanitarian intervention (...). On the other hand, economic issues related to the regulation of world trade saw the United States exercise leadership in promoting trade liberalization, both at the multilateral and bilateral levels".*

As a result, US military and political involvement was critical for the UN to maintain international peace and security. Later, in light of the regional process of trade blocs and political organizations based on multilateralism, the issue of American lead participation will be revisited.

Another important historical point that must be taken into account is the arrival of the 2008 crisis, the most serious since the 1929 Crash that puts in check, once again, the effectiveness of the modus operandi developed after the Bretton Woods agreement, that is, it puts check the mechanism governed by WTO rules.

The 2008 financial crisis was a turning point in foreign relations. It was the culmination of a multilateral stalemate that had lasted for years. It had an impact on discussions about the international system's power distribution as well as international governance mechanisms. The emergence of the crisis highlighted the contradictions of a globalized economy that had experienced decades of asymmetrical growth and, in most cases, had been free of challenges.

> *"The economic crisis that started in 2008 had a peculiarity: it did not occur in developing countries, but in the central countries of capitalism, and with wider proportions and developments. This crisis triggered a process of transformation in the mechanisms of global governance: the loss of legitimacy of the G-8, the expansion of substantive discussions for the G-20 and the strengthening and capitalization of the IMF, although with uncertainties regarding its future role. Thus, on November 15, 2008, the first summit of G-20 leaders took place in Washington and aimed to 'restore global growth' (G-20 2008, $1). How to achieve this broad consensus objective would be a great challenge. (Ramos, Vadell, Saggioro & Fernandes, 2012, p.04)."*

Later on, the historical context that may have triggered the abandonment of multilateral logic in favor of bilateral logic will be detailed a little more and more densely.

For the time being, only the emergence of a new economic and political scenario will be highlighted, as Gama & Camargo (2018) point out, by highlighting the central scenario of the debates of economies that previously orbited on the periphery of the economic scenario of global governance. These countries, which had been operating their own development models for decades, were finally recognized.

THE BREXIT CASE

The International Monetary Fund (IMF) has reduced its forecast for the growth of the world economy in 2020 (IMF, 2020). With British macroeconomic indices falling, the government aims to enter into bilateral trade and investment agreements.

On the other hand, after Greece's moratorium in 2015, the European Union has been facing a major crisis (Gama, 2020) and disagreements over the migration of Syrians that marked the years 2010. The simultaneous search for autonomy and cooperation is one of the paradoxes of the process of globalization, marked mainly by the abandonment of Greece, which was one of the main occurrences responsible for the balance of Europe after the wars of the 19th and 20th century.

The rebellion that started in the Conservative Party ended half a century of history. The unfriendly stance of Donald Tusk, President of the European Commission, facilitated the radical wing of Brexit. The Conservative Party, winner of the general elections in the United Kingdom since 2009, assumed itself as a nationalist party, with the commitment to "get Brexit done".

"From her first statement as Prime Minister, Theresa May made it clear that Brexit marked a break in our politics. Standing outside her new front door on 13 July, she declared her intention to make Britain 'a country that works for everyone', driven by the interests of those 'just about managing' rather than those part of the 'privileged few'. Launching her Plan for Britain in March 2017, she was still more explicit, remarking that the 'EU referendum result was an instruction to change the way our country works, and the people for whom it works forever'. (Evans & Menon, 2017, p.12)."

Brexit not only changed the way the UK would deal with economic policy from then on, but it marked the transition from the logic of the multilateral to the bilateral world forever. The phenomenon was one of the first warnings to transform international relations between countries.

The conclusion of Brexit represents a microcosm of global trends. The conservative government, with no commitment to community norms, promises important economic growth based on trade agreements and flexible environmental standards, selectively restricting the transit of people without a British citizenship. Restriction and commercial agreements, as well as selective restriction of traffic for people who do not have a British citizenship. Thirty years after the fall of the Berlin Wall, the partially globalized world (Keohane, 2002) finds itself entirely closed.

The impact of Brexit resonated around the world. For example, in the United States, the era marked by Trump's populism establishes a la carte negotiations, nationalism and populist leaders with the promise of growth and the exclusion of possible threats.

The WTO remains paralyzed by the supposed disinterest of the United States in appointing new members of its dispute settlement body, a Trump strategy to weaken the Organization, a multilateral trading system, and to bet on bilateral or inter-bloc negotiations - in which the American power has greater bargaining power.

FROM GLOBALIZATION TO BILATERAL AGREEMENTS

As seen so far, the Uruguayan negotiation, the creation of the WTO, the celebration of NAFTA and the establishment of the APC (Asia-Pacific Economic Cooperation Area), show the relevance of the dominance of multilateralism in the world.

> *"However, the USA has also developed a set of bilateral trade liberalization agreements, which signaled some difficulties in maintaining the multilateral approach as a privileged vehicle for these negotiations. (Fernandes & Simão, 2019, p.27)."*

This American strategy of not relying solely on multilateral logic appears to have gained traction in recent years. According to Souza, both developing and developed countries are frustrated by the slow pace of multilateral trade and integration negotiations, which has resulted in an unprecedented increase in parallel agreements. (2008).

The signing of bilateral investment agreements has gained traction around the world over time. The bilateral agreements, or BITs, of the English Bilateral Investment Treaty have gained force since the first term was signed by Germany and Pakistan in 1959. Many bilateral agreements are currently in force between countries all over the world.

According to Wei (2010), as globalization becomes more profound and the internationalization of companies is accelerating, BITS, undergoing some innovations, are already part of the international regime in terms of investments and have an important role in fixing rules for the treatment of foreign capital. We consider bilateral investment protection and promotion agreement to be a pact aimed at establishing terms and conditions for investors in the receiving State

> *"Typically, in most bilateral investment treaties, typical content covers the definition of foreign investment, the conditions for entry of foreign investment into the host country (through the admission clause or the right of establishment), treatment for foreign investors (either the absolute criterion treatment, through the fair and equitable treatment clause, or the relative criterion treatment, through the most favored nation and national treatment clauses), legal limits of expropriation and nationalization, as well as the indemnity standards , the transfer (remittance) of the ownership of foreign investments (capital and profits) and the dispute settlement mechanism between foreign investors and the host state on investment issues (Sennes, 2003, p. 44)."*

It is critical to recognize that the logic of bilateralism finds support in even the most basic negotiations and the consolidation of formally approved and homogenized agreements between trade blocs or countries. It has gained traction in recent years, perhaps as a result of this agreement.

> *"Bilateral relations (...) were guided by two strategic objectives: to seek alternatives to "special" relations with the United States through the approximation of Western Europe and Japan; and to expand relations with different countries in*

the Third World, presenting itself as an alternative to the great powers (Sennes, 2003, p.45)."

Therefore, it can be considered that the process of signing bilateral investment treaties was born, mainly, as a response by investors from developed countries to the nationalization movements that took place in developing countries and to the appeals of these countries ensured by the multilateral instrument - the Charter of Social Economic Rights and Duties of States (United Nations Resolution No. 3281 of 1974). In order to seek a new international regime, developed countries strongly promoting the BIT's negotiations.

In its 2007 annual report, the United Nations Commission on Trade and Development points out that the bilateral agreements signed by smaller countries with the United States or developed countries with developing countries are dangerous. Which refers to the discomfort that this possibility brings to the context of multilateralism.

According to Souza (2008, not paginated), in the approach of the aforementioned report, Bilateral agreements are attempts by developed countries to sign agreements in areas of mutual interest, and they may stymie Mercosur integration efforts. The document "raises the possibility that this strategy may not be the best in the long run." On the other hand, it says,

> *"The work raises a range of issues related to regional integration, especially regarding what is called new regionalism, which is not necessarily done between countries that are in the same region, but between countries that have common interests, although being geographically distant. (Souza, 2008, not paginated)".*

Generally, developed countries offer the advantage of access to their markets, and demand in return, an agreement. Developing countries that bet on bilateral agreements usually make larger concessions on terms. Far beyond the concessions they would make in multilateral agreements. This makes countries more vulnerable in this relationship.

A PATH TO THE LOGIC OF BILATERALISM

Over the last few years, the US, in particular, has quietly embraced a political strategy that views bilateralism as a complementary path to the consolidated multilateralist structure in trade blocs and global political organizations.

Let us consider, in the perspective of this work, that the United States has made a broad effort to expand its engagement in Latin America.

> *"South American countries, for their part, maintained very close ties with the United Kingdom, which translated, in part, into a more cautious attitude towards the US attempts to foster pacts and agreements that span the entire continent, especially through part of Argentina. The relative stability achieved by Argentina, Brazil and Chile is another aspect to be considered, as it "allowed the development of a regional subsystem right at the beginning of the political life of those States. (Teixeira, 2014, p. 123)."*

The United States understanding of this search for hegemony in the American continent is extremely relevant because it presents the strategic scenario that may have stimulated the country to maintain and, more recently, foster the priority of bilateralism in relation to multilateralism.

> *"Initiatives such as the construction of the Panama Canal, interventionism in Cuba, and the maintenance of Puerto Rico as a protectorate, illustrate the concentration of US activism in the central portion of the American continent, until at least the 1930s. However, the expansion of the country's power and presence on the continent as a whole has become a goal of increasing relevance as the US international agenda has become more complex and diverse. (Donadelli & Pereira, 2019, p.175)."*

From the findings of the authors who have supported this study so far, it can be inferred that over the past few years, the United States has adopted an ambiguous logic - one publicly declared: that of multilateralism and another that is subliminal and strategic: that of bilateralism, which before, however, it operated as a subliminal parallel form in the global political and economic context. The goal of this research is to see if the logic stated in the case study is still valid at this time.

> *"The responses formulated by the United States in this scenario were based on a post-Cold World view crystallized under the rubric of 'New World Order'. President George H. Bush coined the term in 1990, and its meaning referred to the concept of a "liberal pax" characterized by the rule of law, cooperation, and the avoidance of violent conflict resolution. In the case of regional security, the widespread notion was "Cooperative Security", which became terminology used in the Conferences of Ministers of Defense of the Americas (CMDA). (Donadelli & Pereira, 2019, p.182)."*

This finding reveals an American tactic that, as previously mentioned, may have helped the country to gain more relevance throughout history in the UN and the WTO, based on this concept of 'Cooperative Security'. An assumption of domination that has been consolidated over the years.

> *"From then, through mutually agreed mechanisms, the interested countries would work together to' ensure regional stability '"* (Abdul-Hak, 2013, p.212). *Under the argument of international cooperation to face the new threats and phenomena resulting from globalization, the new concept was linked to effective institutions with a multilateral seal (Rojas, 1999, p.19)."*

Undoubtedly a strategy of silent domination that has altered the global paradigm and which may be the source of the fear and institutional insecurity that hangs over countries, as will be discussed in the next chapter, and which serves as a stimulus for the rise of bilateral agreements at the expense of multilateralist logic.

In practice, this paradigm established a set of actions aimed at the exchange of military information, with the objective of building trust and transparency (Vitelli, 2018). In this sense, cooperative security has resulted in an attempt to establish a regional order capable of prolonging US supremacy - no longer through coercion or the threat of nuclear deterrence, but through its acceptance by countries in the region (Pinto, 2015, p. .46).

It will be urgent to consider a possible concept of bilateralism in the scope of this research. Evidently, there are innumerable conceptual paths that are being listed by several researchers. Here, the concept of bilateralism supported by the Realistic International Relations theory fits very wel,l presented by Morgenthau (1997, cited by Pontes, 2016, p.10),

"This time, unlike at the endogenous level, where the State has a normative framework and a legal monopoly of force, at the international level, power and reason lead realists to assert that states moved along the international path in a continuous search for the realization of their national interests, which are defined in terms of power, regardless of the ultimate purpose that each nation wants to attribute to it - alteration of the status quo, maintenance or prestige, where no world authority or government is envisioned that oppose them."

This will therefore be the scenario on which the bilateral plan to be considered will be developed. An atmosphere of relations between countries that continue their relations with each other in isolation, in parallel to the multilateral order now in force. It is important to conceive that one phenomenon is not isolated from the other, they occur in parallel and are opposed more intensely from the strengthening of one in relation to the other. To this end, the position of Magalhães (1996, p.70) will be followed, by which he perceives that bilateralism translates the international contact between two States.

CASE STUDY: A MAP FROM MULTILATERALISM TO BILATERALISM

The reinforcement of a new, bilateralism logic is investigated, in the scope of world commercial relations. It will be tried to infer if, based on this logic, there are interferences in the main world organizations that have guided multilateralism until now.

On one hand, all studies of the WTO, its assemblies and the new rules of trade established (and often unfulfilled), demonstrate that there is an emptying of the organizations responsible for multilateralism, as is the case of the WTO itself and the UN.

Internal pressures from capitalist elites (independent variable) may be in line with socialism with Chinese characteristics and the effect of this would be a tendency towards bilateralism in the agreements. In effect, a protectionist response could be a return to nationalist ideas, emptying universal multilateralism and opening space for regional interests, concluded in bilateral agreements (dependent variable), as will be explained below.

Global economic groups have become independent from the interests of nations. They started to have their own agenda of interest. They became supranational entities and moved away from their countries of origin. These groups sought development sites that, in the first place, avoided taxation and exempted taxes on operations carried out outside the country. And, secondly, in the commercial aspect, they sought that the revenues obtained by them could be reinvested in favor of companies and not in favor of their original countries.

As a result, these companies began to target and hire labor outside their countries of origin to obtain cheaper products and subsequently higher profit margins. In the USA, for example, this practice also generated only a consumer audience for its products. Resulting in the opposition to the national interest of the country's workers created in an independent manner. Logically, the interest of companies was to profit for themselves. Hence the process of job transfers. These groups then started to have conflicting interests with the USA.

For this same reason, the current American government has created conditions to attract companies from outside the country to the American domestic environment and foster job creation in the USA. This phenomenon may have caused an emptying of multilateralism, since the groups were against the American ideal. The country therefore had to regain control in order to defend its interests.

Having said that, it should be noted that the WTO agenda has remained stagnant since its inception in 2001. The European Union's continued expansion, as well as the US-led NAFTA and TPP agreements, as well as bilateral agreements between the US and the European Union and their partners, exemplified this phenomenon.

Thus, what is perceived is that in the last two decades, bilateral and regional trade agreements have been considered a primary force to advance the world trade system, making the WTO meetings empty and generating serious challenges with the increase of multilateralist anti-globalization sentiment.

In June 2016, the United Kingdom decided to leave the EU as a result of a referendum. On January 23, 2017, right at the beginning of his presidency, Donald Trump signed the withdrawal of the U.S. from the TPP as his first executive order, an agreement signed with 11 more partners than his predecessor, who took years to complete it.

These two dramatic actions shocked the world. Alongside the WTO, regionalism is seen as the second best choice in promoting globalization, but these regional initiatives led by developed countries are facing a serious reaction. The world is concerned that this will mean the end or a reversal of the process of Multilateralist Globalization.

An important historical point that is being considered was the action of the European Parliament and the Council, on a proposal from the Commission, which issued Regulation No. 1219/2012 on December 12, 2012, establishing transitional provisions for bilateral investment agreements between States, Member States and third world countries.

At the same time, in point 8 it is stated that "this Regulation should also lay down the conditions under which Member States are empowered to conclude and / or maintain in force the bilateral investment agreements signed between 1 December 2009 and 9 January 2013".

To that end, "States must remove the incompatibilities between bilateral investment agreements and Union law", in accordance with point 12 of the Regulation.

The understanding of this assumption in the EU, ensures an attempt to standardize and regulate the origins of bilateral agreements in terms formerly not observed historically. A release by the member states to agree on bilateral agreements that are of interest as a legal presupposition in this matter.

The following section of the regulation is regarded as a critical component that justifies the legal conclusion of bilateral agreements between countries during the administration of the multilateralist assumption that has governed international relations to this point. The excerpt from the Regulation highlights: "this time, if EU Member States want authorization to conclude bilateral investment agreements, the provisions of Articles 8 to 11 of the above-mentioned Regulation must be verified, namely in the following articles":

> *"Art. 9: The Commission authorizes Member States to initiate official negotiations with a third country, in order to amend or conclude a bilateral investment agreement, except in cases where it considers that the opening of such negotiations*

may: a) Collide with the Union law, in aspects other than incompatibilities arising from the division of competences between the Union and its Member States; (b) be redundant, since the Commission has submitted or has decided to submit, in accordance with Article 218 (3) TFEU, a recommendation to open negotiations with the third world country concerned; c) Be incompatible with the Union's principles and objectives for external action established in accordance with the general provisions set out in Title V, Chapter 1, of the Treaty on European Union; (d) constitute a serious obstacle to the negotiation or conclusion by the Union of bilateral investment agreements with third world countries. (Regulation (EU) No. 1219/2012, p.42)."

Another important point of this regulation is the:

paragraph 2: "in the context of the authorization referred to in paragraph 1, the Commission may require the Member State to either participate or not from these negotiations and the bilateral investment agreement provided for all clauses, if necessary, in order to ensure consistency with the Union's investment policy or compatibility with Union law; Article 9 (5): "if the Commission decides not to grant the authorization provided for in paragraph 1, it shall inform the Member State concerned accordingly, stating the reasons for the refusal"; art. 11 (1): "before signing a bilateral investment agreement, the Member State concerned shall notify the Commission of the outcome of the negotiations and forward the text of such an agreement to it"; art. 11 (4): "if the Commission considers that the negotiations have resulted in a bilateral investment agreement that meets the requirements referred to in article

9, paragraphs 1 and 2, it authorizes the Member State to sign and conclude such an agreement"; art. 11 (6): "if the Commission decides to grant an authorization in accordance with paragraph 4, the Member State concerned shall notify the Commission of the conclusion and entry into force of the bilateral investment agreement, and subsequent amendments the status of that agreement "; art. 11 (8): "if the Commission decides not to grant authorization under paragraph 4, it shall inform the Member State concerned accordingly, stating the reasons for the refusal" (Regulation (EU) No 1219 / 2012, p.43).

Thus, based on the investigation proposed in the hypothesis, the objective is to identify the points of support of the old world economy - and how it is reinforced - and the strength points of the new format. Until now, there have been no indications that there is a new, more pulsating stimulus to the bilateralism logic of world trade agreements, to the detriment of the dominant multilateralist logic.

There are sufficient subsidies to consider that bilateral trade agreements are being signed between countries, despite the legal regimentation of the blocks and multilateralist organizations' normative guidelines in many cases.

The only object of study in this study is the bilateral agreements reached in the United States during the administrations of President Barack Obama and President Donald Trump. However, based on the theoretical course and data survey, it appears that the practice of bilateral agreements is widespread around the world, with a higher prevalence in the United States.

This situation merits the following consideration: Agreements are easier in England because there are no significant tariff restrictions; however, in countries like Brazil, which has a highly protected industry, there will be enormous resistance to free trade between two countries through bilateral agreements where the numbers are evident. Therefore, the acceptance of this change will vary from country to country according to the productivity of each one.

In the case of the USA, there is still uncertainty in the future political scenario due to the electoral dispute that may change the course of trade relations, which now continue to move towards bilateral agreements, but which, depending on the decision at the polls, may generate a movement return to the roots of globalization with regard to multilateral agreements.

BACKGROUND CONDITIONS OF THE ANALYSIS

A New Globalization? End of Geopolitics?

What is being investigated is the possibility of changing the current order of multilateralist globalization. An assumption that has already been proven to be real from the theoretical path previously undertaken. Later on, when the case is studied, it will be seen that this hypothesis is already real and that a new legal and diplomatic order may be in progress for this new era, which is more bilateralist than multilateralist in the world market.

> *"The heterogeneity of these groups represents an obstacle in the attempt to characterize them under a single conceptual key. However, the following set of characteristics can be highlighted in common: greater permeability to a critical discourse of unilateralism and economic-financial establishment recommendations; reverberation of autonomous affirmation speeches and defense of regional integration, in different shades. (Donadelli & Pereira, 2019, p.185)."*

There is, as seen, a certain implicit regularity in the conclusion of bilateral agreements between countries. In other words, the logic is the same (bilateral), but the modus operandis abides by the policies and ideologies of each country.

Currently, the United States is rapidly transforming into a radiating pole for global economic policy dictates. By allowing profits earned by American companies operating abroad to enter the country, President Trump has turned the country into a major offshore, depending on the agreements, without tax, in the non-tariff heading. This completely changed American politics, bringing back the interest of large American conglomerates based abroad.

Therefore, the great ambition of multilateralist globalization to make a world free of borders has been diminishing little by little giving way to the bilateral agreements that have been defining the new format of world trade.

Thus, new economic and legal perspectives arise from the deceleration of multilateralism and the development of agreements based solely on bilateral interests.

Both nations, populations, and individuals on the globe have gradually become part of a global society in the last two decades of the twentieth century. However, since the World Trade Organization - WTO - was founded, things have changed. The fundamentals of the globalization process have experienced drastic shifts in the light of all the changes in the world situation, which have not been converted into new laws at the same rate as they seem.

This transformation process has been putting the WTO on the margins and weakening government structures, as it motivates States to solve regulatory problems arising from regional or bilateral free trade agreements.

After a certain time, it became increasingly clear that there was an exhaustion of the processes of globalization because the rules created to manage it did not protect the parties in an equal way.

Both developing and developed countries are frustrated by the slow rounds of multilateral negotiations on trade and integration, and this has led to an unprecedented growth in parallel agreements, according to Souza (2008).

The process of signing bilateral investment treaties arose primarily as a response by investors from developed countries to nationalization movements in developing countries, as well as to the appeals of these countries guaranteed by the multilateral instrument. - the Charter of Social Economic Rights and Duties of States (Resolution United Nations Organization No. 3281 of 1974).

In this new scenario, it is necessary to analyze the phenomenon of transition from multilateralism in trade relations to new ways of conducting economic and international policies in the world economic aspects. It is possible that the new globalization is being structured by the way in which bilateral agreements are being carried out today.

There is a notable decrease in multilateral meetings at the WTO, which leads to the assertion that there is a transformation of the globalization process in return for a significant increase in bilateral agreements. As a result, in order to survive, the globalization process must adapt to a new form of negotiation that prioritizes bilateralism.

In this context, the tendency of the United States as a probable promoter of the new economic world order based on bilateral agreements brings to light the most recent agreements signed by that country in this bipolar format and elucidates the diminishing power of international commercial, military and health organizations.

The movement to reduce meetings at the WTO, with a view to increase the conclusion of bilateral agreements between countries, shows a trend towards the establishment of a new world economic order that comes to significantly transform the globalization process, initially based on multilateral treaties that can no longer serve the interests of all countries. The influence of this change on the world's political and commercial scenario will ultimately define the world's economic future and new trade relations.

The phenomenon of an increase in bilateral agreements, which generates the emptying of WTO meetings, indicates an ontological change in the globalization process. It can be seen that since its launch in 2001, the WTO agenda has in fact been stagnant. The continuous expansion of the European

Union, NAFTA and the TPP - led by the USA -, as well as the bilateral agreements between the USA and the European Union and their partners exemplified this phenomenon well.

In the past two decades, bilateral and regional trade agreements have been seen as a primary force to advance the world trade system, generating serious challenges with the increase in anti-globalization sentiment.

In June 2016, the United Kingdom left the EU as a result of a referendum. On January 23, 2017, Donald Trump signed his first executive order as president, withdrawing the United States from the Trans-Pacific Partnership (TPP), a deal signed with 11 more allies than his predecessor, which took years to achieve.

These two dramatic actions shocked the world. Alongside the WTO, regionalism is seen as the second best choice in promoting globalization, but these regional initiatives led by developed countries are facing a serious reaction. The world is concerned that this will mean the end or a reversal of the globalization process,

> With regard to bilateral relations in the post-Cold War period, we to identify gradients of acquiescence in the US security policies with the countries of the region, with Colombia and Venezuela occupying the contrasting extremes of such logic (...) what can be inferred from this period is the existence of a pattern of performance that, although it has not entirely dispensed with multilateralism, it has been based mainly on bilateral channels of action. (Donadelli & Pereira, 2019, p.189)."

Given this situation, it's also important to call attention to the less expensive factors that might encourage countries, especially the United States, to sign more bilateral agreements and expand multilateralism across the board: the financial economy.

> "This situation can be attributed to the combination of the US security agenda in the period with the regional political situation. In a scenario of greater attention to the strategic theater of the Middle East, of which the leaders of the main Latin American countries were unwilling to accept uncritical adherence to American designs, the bilateral route appears to be an effective path and with the lowest political cost in the country. than the costly process of sewing consensus at the continental level. (Donadelli & Pereira, 2019, p.190)."

Following, another relevant historical moment that needs to be considered in this analysis will be presented: the trade war between China and the USA.

CHINA – U.S TRADE WAR: THE STANDARDS FOR GLOBAL CHANGE

The world saw the multilateral trading system's hegemony challenged in 2018 by unilateral decisions by the United States regarding the taxation of Chinese products. The increase in the country's trade deficit in recent years served as justification for the American country.

In 2017, the United States identified a deficit of US $ 861 billion in the trade balance of goods, against US $ 797 billion in 2016. In 2017, there was an increase in the bilateral deficit with China by 7%, reaching US $ 363 billion, equivalent to 42% of the total deficit (COMTRADE, 2018).

The public reciprocal trade agenda of Donald Trump, president of the United States, came into effect in his first months of his government. The reports in Sections 232 (on investigating the effect of aluminum and steel imports on national security) and 301 (identifying trade barriers to US products and companies) were the basis for his unilateral decisions. China was chosen as a priority country in 2018 due to intellectual property laws and a list of countries to be investigated as a priority.

In the final report of the investigation carried out by the US Trade Representative's Office[1], under Section 232 of the Trade Expansion Act of 1962, and delivered on January 11, 2018 to President Trump, it was found that "the quantities and circumstances of steel and aluminum imports threaten to undermine national security ".

The agency suggested a tariff imposition of 24% on all steel products in all countries and 7.7% on all aluminum products in all countries (USTR, 2018). In another completed investigation, the Cabinet in April 2018 released trade restrictions practiced by China.

Donald Trump attributed the great deficit of the United States to the unfair commercial practices of the communist regime, such as currency war through currency devaluation in the long run, violation of patent and intellectual property rights, reduction of wages, dumping, tax incentives for exporting companies, subsidized interest for investment in industry and protectionist measures.

On March 8, 2018, President Donald Trump, following the recommendations of the Office of the Commercial Representative on Section 232, signed a regulation setting an additional 10% on aluminum for all countries and 25% on the value of tax on aluminum. Steel imports. In April 2018, Trump also announced, starting from Section 301, a list of products from China that would be surcharged, at the equivalent of $ 50 billion, on imports.

Then, also in March 2018, China notified the World Trade Organization (WTO) of retaliation measures directed at the USA, imposing import tariffs

---

1   USTR

on several products imported from that country, including soybeans, whose imposed tariff was 25%[2].

A historical note is necessary in this context. After 2008, China has reached the top of industrial economies. President Barack Obama was elected in the United States with a promise to bring the American economy back on track, but he has not been able to fully achieve his goals. Later, the challenged United States elected a real estate tycoon who drifted away from international norms towards protectionism.

In the trade war that started, China aimed at the agricultural sector and the USA at the Chinese industrial sector. This unprecedented reversal in the role puts the southern hemisphere at the helm of a change in the world order (Gama & Camargo, 2018).

With a government-controlled economy, China gradually evolved into a backbone that merged regional production chains in a type of integration that was far less reliant on normative rules than in Europe.

An example of such pragmatism is the Chinese concept of "duojihua", translated by Li (2002), a term defined by Li (2002) as "multi-polarization" or "asymmetric diplomacy". In contrast to Western concepts, duojihua asserts that there is no hegemony or predominance of a single nation in the world, and that all countries play a role in the system.

Duojihua also invokes a stance of tolerance and understanding between different cultures and policies. China, and other BRICS, also substitute market forces for the State as the driver of transitions in globalization "liberalization under the rules of the State" (Jain, 2006).

By investing in bilateral negotiations with recalcitrant allies bursting "new" markets for US products, Trump basically replicates the Chinese strategy.

---

2   In June 2018, the European Union (EU) followed suit and reported its retaliatory measures to the WTO.

It appears to balance the game at first glance, but in a world of competitive scarcity, it may have dark implications with other business partners.

According to Araújo (2019), the USA, given the international negotiation strategy that the Trump Administration has been adopting, signed new terms with Canada and Mexico under the North American Free Trade Agreement (NAFTA). In addition to traditional commercial issues, this change in the NAFTA agreement stands out, the reinforcement and updating of important issues such as, for example, Intellectual Property, which has a special chapter focused on Digital Trade.

It is important to highlight that, both the United States and the European countries (European Union and EFTA), present greater prominence in terms of numbers of trade preference agreements. In developing countries, compared to developed countries, advances are relatively minor, with some exceptions, such as China. The increasing importance of the digital economy will affect trade patterns and the way trade agreements are established.

Four top priorities of the new United States trade policy can be highlighted, in a clear departure from multilateral trade rules, according to ENAP (2014):

- defend national sovereignty over trade policy;

- strictly enforce US trade laws;

- ensure that other countries open their markets for the export of goods and services, in order to guarantee the protection of the intellectual property rights of US companies;

- negotiate "new and better" trade agreements with the country and without interference of "key markets" worldwide.

As a concrete and definitive act of the new government with a wide scope in terms of trade policy, we can mention as an example the withdrawal of the United States from the Trans-Pacific Partnership (TPP), the abandonment of the Transatlantic Partnership (TTIP) negotiations with the European Union

(EU) and the announcement of the terms for the renegotiation of the North American Free Trade Agreement (NAFTA), mentioned above.

The Paris Agreement (2015) - a milestone in global cooperation to combat climate change - faces considerable casualties, such as that of Trump's USA, in addition to the resistance of emerging countries such as Australia, Brazil and India. The Global Pact for Migration (2018) faces resistance from nationalists and populists, in a world where walls have proliferated again (Niblett & Bhardwaj, 2019).

As a result, in light of the need for greater integration with international trade policies, rethinking the form of elaboration of public policies aimed at the productive sector becomes critical in the context of global productive transformations.

In order to reduce the deficit with China, the United States imposed a tax on Chinese steel and aluminum. The rule authorizes taxes on 1,300 products originating in China. This American measure clearly violates WTO rules. They affect exports from another member country of the Organization.

The Chinese response came quickly. The eastern power government also announced the imposition of tariffs on more than 100 American products.

In this sense, the United States' trade protectionism and China's retaliatory actions may affect the export of related products on the Brazilian export agenda. In 2017, Chinese soy imports accounted for 60% of total soy sales on the world market, with Brazil being one of the largest suppliers of this product to the Asian market.

According to the new tariffs, the Ministry of Commerce of China predicts that part of the market supplied by the United States will be more occupied by Brazilian products because China intends to impose a 25% import tariff on US soybeans, a product in which Brazil has been taking the lead in world exports in recent years.

Another product that when affected by tariffs can change the intersectional allocation is steel, as 9% of the US $ / FOB exports of 2017 were iron and concentrates, which includes steel (MDIC, 2018). Through a computable general equilibrium model, this work seeks to identify the effects of a possible war between its largest trading partners in the main sectors of the economy in Brazil.

A summary of the main tariff measures adopted by China and the United States, the object of this study, is presented in Table 1. The USA determines the tariffs for steel and aluminum to be applied to trading partners. The trade dispute between these two countries affects 1,363 products, which is equivalent to US $ 34 million for each of them.

Table 1 - Main tariff measures in China and the United States

Products	Country adopting tariff measure	Ad valorem Import tariff	Affected countries
Steel	U.S	25%	SEVERAL
Aluminum	U.S	10%	SEVERAL
American list with 818 Chinese products	U.S	25%	CHINA
Chinese list with 545 American products	CHINA	25%	U.S

Source: Carvalho, Azevedo & Massuquete, 2019, p.04.

Tariffs on steel and aluminum will be imposed on a global scale in order to guarantee national security and impose tariffs on the United States, according to the measures taken by the United States in the first phase of the trade war. Steel and aluminum provide services to the following economic partners: Brazil (which decided to set the highest export quota), Argentina, Mexico and Canada, the last two countries formed after the renegotiation of the North American Free Trade Agreement.

To combat excess Chinese production capacity, reduce the country's deficit in the trade balance and as a way to offset issues related to US intellectual property and technology, the USA released a list of 818 Chinese products that would cover 25% of additional import tariff (USTR, 2018).

On June 7th, 2018. The charge on these imports took effect and a total of $ 34 billion was attributed to imports from China. Products included in the list: vehicles, medical and precision instruments, hard drives, radio transmitters, nuclear reactors, water heaters, tires and aircraft parts.

In response, China retaliated to the U.S. with a list of 545 US products for a total of $ 34 billion in imports (MOFCOM, 2018). The list includes vehicles, agricultural products and food.

This scenario leads us to a conflict that is far from over and that can increasingly stimulate the opening of bilateral trade agreements in the global context. An economic dispute, but above all, a policy that is already, as we have seen, opening a new commercial horizon far beyond multilateralism worldwide.

A New Diplomacy

Understanding the above-mentioned new context, which is currently in full swing, we seek to focus in a concise manner on this topic, on how the diplomatic institution has sought to exercise its function as a mechanism for peaceful State contact throughout history. It aims to determine whether the context studied has influenced and will continue to influence the structure of world diplomacy and its performance along this path,

> *"Therefore, looking at this situation, it is important to mention that we maintain that diplomatic activity, more specifically Diplomatic Negotiation itself, it can act in accordance with the two dimensions dealt with in this investigation: the Bilateral - State to State - the Multilateral - which checks within the IOs, to a large extent, by way of example, with regard to regulatory agreements, such as those that we can verify through the GATT / WTO rounds. (Pontes, 2016, p. 230)."*

Regardless of the subject at hand, in order to better comprehend how the diplomatic institution's performance has gradually been affirming an increasingly economic component of its international contacts, particularly bilateral ones, it is necessary, first and foremost, to seek out what has been doctrinally understood by diplomacy, following Magalhães' position. (1996).

According to this author, diplomacy, in its purest state, should be distinguished from all elements that have nothing to do with diplomatic activity, being understood as "a foreign policy instrument for establishing and developing peaceful contacts between the governments of different states through the use of mutually recognized intermediaries," which can translate into bilateral or multilateral contacts. (Magalhães, 1996, p.90).

This understanding ensures that diplomacy, in one of its possible conceptual sketches, can and should act much more linked to the bilateralism logic than the already consolidated multilateralist one. A new presupposition of action should be studied and understood by diplomatic bodies all over the world, with the goal of moving the debate on global geo-economic, political, and climatic issues to a more regionalized sphere guided by common interests between countries.

> "As the number of states multiplies and their ability to interact increases, based on what principles can a new world order emerge? With the complexity of the new system, can concepts such as 'expanding democracy' serve as a guideline for American foreign policy and as a substitute for the Cold War containment policy? (Kissinger, 2012, p.182)."

The concept of a new world order defended and applied by the post-Cold War United States may be getting supplanted by a new, more silent strategy, based on bilateralism as a form of trade expansion and a more progressive and fierce economic vision between countries. In this context, there will be a total impact on the structure of Global Diplomacy that should be ready for this new phenomenon.

Therefore, according to Farto's (2006) view, three extremely relevant axes on the model of diplomacy that we are dealing with in this research can be identified: economic diplomacy.

The author translates three axes for Economic Diplomacy and considers it: "the security action where the political objectives are dominant, the regulatory action where the two orders of objectives come together and the competitive action of clear economic dominance" (Farto, 2006, p.67).

> "In the first case, the aforementioned author refers to diplomatic action in the context of regional integration - first of all because the provisions such as the Internal Market, Agriculture and fisheries, Energy and economic, social and territorial Cohesion, which comprise economic domains, represent matters of competence. shared in accordance with art. 4, paragraph 2 of the TFEU - insofar as it can serve to speculate or assert the position of a Member State. Simultaneously, the first axis points us to the cases "in which the intervention of economic diplomacy seeks to contribute to a solution, supporting or economically sanctioning one or more parties in conflict. (Farto, 2006, p. 12)."

In this context, not only does diplomacy lose the character of a peaceful instrument of the EP, getting into the category of violent, according to Magalhães (1996, p.25), as it is often diminished, since the power to interrupt or to totally or partially reduce economic and financial relations with third countries belongs to the Union (Article 215 (1) TFEU). In both cases, the objectives to be pursued by diplomacy are eminently political.

"The second axis relates to regulatory action that is exercised at the multilateral level, largely through participation in international bodies such as the WTO, verifying a double political and economic character, and through these actions, [that] economic diplomacy organizes the transfer of international and regional powers, since national States have lost the exclusive control over their economic and social processes. (Farto, 2006, p.12)."

Despite the fact that national states, as Farto (2006, p.12) shows, have "still high margins of responsibility, ranging from the use of budgetary means to the preservation of social cohesion", in a multilateral context of regulatory action, diplomacy's anachronism may become increasingly diminished. This aids in determining whether EU Member States have lost their relevance in terms of regulating international trade.

Finally, with regard to the competitive action axis,

"It mainly refers to the creation of a competitive State and to the support of national companies operating in the international sphere. Thus, through the scope of its activities, a coordinated and integrated strategy between the objectives of the State and the action of the private sector is privileged, with a view to granting favorable internal conditions for the dynamic of the economy, in conjunction with action in the field bilateral agreement of the State's diplomatic apparatus. (Farto, 2006, p.13)."

As previously stated, while the diplomatic institution continues to operate in the context of world integration and economic regulation in the context of the WTO, multilateral economic diplomacy has been losing ground as a result of the movements of European countries, particularly the pressure exerted by the US in this context.

As a result, the major axis of national state action in the context of Economic Diplomacy, in its broadest sense, as well as the use of the diplomatic corps, in particular, for economic purposes, should emerge from multilaterality and continue to be better adapted to the logic of commercial bilateralism.

Possible Micro-cases

At this point in the work, it is very important to assess, in addition to the background conditions presented above, possible micro-causes that have motivated the occurrence of the American commercial transition (scenario of the object of study of this project) from the multilateral logic to the bilateral dimension.

1) Nationalist sentiment gains strength in the society

In 1980, observing the American middle class from that time, it had a standard of living in the social context very close to that of Brazil with regard to quality of life and the configuration of work within the family nucleus. Usually, in this period, only one person worked to support the home. Over time, the couple began to work to maintain the same standard of living.

Currently, at least one member of the family works in more than one job to support the household. This is a strong indication that can prove the eventual fall of the purchasing power of the American middle class.

This new American middle class is currently under pressure from large corporations and the transfer of part of their jobs abroad. This could be one of the micro-causes that led to political change and the emergence of ultranationalist sentiment, which could have been used by current President Donald Trump, in addition to electing himself, to base his speech on the use of this phenomenon to anchor a more bilateral logic in shaping the American commercial relationship during his term.

It is essential to consider that this micro-cause can also be observed in other countries of the world, which reinforces the thesis that it may be one of the important reasons for the transition of this scenario from multi to bilateralism in the commercial and political field.

2) BETWEEN HEGEMONIES AND OLIGOPOLIES: THE CHINESE METHOD THAT SCARES

As seen, the post-cold war generated a crisis in the current model of hegemony. Countries had to redesign this phenomenon, especially the United States, which has always sought to be a protagonist in this issue.

In the 21st century, the United States sought to reorganize its hegemony over other countries in the international system. After the 2008 crisis, China initiated an expansion process, aiming to overcome its position as an adjunct of capitalism vis-à-vis the USA.

The country that sought to be more autonomous and assertive, began to fight for the control of technology, develop brands and conquer markets to stop the organization and centralize global value chains. Another strategy used by the Chinese was to try to move up the international labor hierarchy in order to gain a larger share of the added value.

There is a construction of a new China with the clear intention of placing itself as a military power and technology leader, in addition to maintaining itself worldwide as a manufacturing and economic power. This strong movement of capitalist expansion puts the country in control of technological practices, making it a net exporter of capital and, at the same time, with acquisitions and mergers that guarantee the supply of energy and food.

As seen, in the background that was dealt with in the trade war between the US vs. China, the United States, in particular under the management of Donald Trump, is looking to hinder this Chinese rise. The goal is to define policies to strengthen multinationals and weaken Chinese oligopolies.

We can observe then, a struggle aimed at dominating the new technological revolution, involving competition between oligopolies and the dispute between more developed countries. Thus, it is observed that interstate rivalry (between countries) mixes with oligopolistic competition.

In the end, the industrial-technological base determines the position of world governments in the hierarchy of the interstate system. In other words, instead of just following, from afar, this scenario of trade war between the two major powers in the world, Western countries are looking to defend themselves against this Chinese oligopoly that partially destroyed the Western productive system.

This too, can be considered a micro-cause for the transition from the multi scenario to commercial bilateralism. Since countries, especially Western countries, are eager to obtain advantages that arise in the midst of this conflict.

3) POWER RETURNS TO COUNTRIES: THE WEAKENING OF WORLD ECONOMIC GROUPS

At this point, it is considered that there is a global transition that seeks to limit the power of the economic groups that gradually dominated the global economy and returns the decision-making power to the hands of the countries in isolation. A fundamental logic that can prove the possible rise of bilateralism and abrupt abandonment to the multilateralist commercial model.

In the USA, under the administration of President Donald Trump, a bilateral agreement strategy with richer countries is observed, that is, there is a greater willingness of these countries to negotiate in isolation and outside the multilateral terms previously considered to be predominant. This can be a clear reason that supports the paradigm that is investigated in this project

STUDYING AMERICAN TRADE AGREEMENTS AND APPLYING THE METHODOLOGY

The United States currently has free trade agreements in place with 20 countries. These are: Australia, Bahrain, Canada, Chile, Colombia, Costa Rica, Dominican Republic, El Salvador, Guatemala, Honduras, Israel, Jordan, Korea, Mexico, Morocco, Nicaragua, Oman, Panama, Peru and Singapore. The following American trade agreements follow:

TRANS-PACIFIC FREE TRADE AGREEMENT

Signed in 1994, the parties, in accordance with Article XXIV of GATT 1994 and Article V of GATS, established a free trade area in accordance with the provisions of the multilateral agreement exhibiting a comprehensive regional agreement and promoting economic integration to free trade and investment, bringing economic growth and social benefits, creating new opportunities for workers and businesses, contributing to raise living standards, benefiting consumers, reduce poverty and promote sustainable growth.

Countries that signed this agreement: Australia, Japan, Canada, Brunei, United States, Singapore, Vietnam, Mexico, New Zealand, Malaysia, Chile and Peru. The table below shows the application of the categories of this agreement:

Table 2 - Trans-Pacific Free Trade Agreement

Trans-Pacific Free Trade Agreement	
Nature of the Agreement	Multilateral
Date and Repercussion	Effective from 1994. The agreement represented a milestone in the commercial history of the American continent.
Breakdown of Multilateralist logic	The logic of multilateralism was not broken.
Adoption of the Bilateralism logic	There was no adoption, either in full or in part, of the Bilateralist logic.
General Conclusion	NAFTA represented a historic moment for foreign trade on the American continent. In addition to regulating and promoting trade between the countries of North America, the agreement served as a reference basis for the formatting of other agreements on the continent, such as MERCOSUR.

Source: Prepared by the Author (2020).

CHILE'S FREE TRADE AGREEMENT

The United States-Chile Free Trade Agreement (LAC) entered into force on January 1, 2004. The United States-Chile LAC eliminates tariffs and opens markets, reduces barriers to trade in services, offers protection of intellectual property, ensures transparency regulations, guarantees non-discrimination in the trade of digital products commits the Parties to maintain competition laws that prohibit anti-competitive business conduct and requires effective environmental and labor standards. With the twelfth annual tariff reduction in effect on January 1, 2015, 100% of US exports will enter Chile tax free. Below, in Table 4, the application of the researched categories:

Table 4 - Chile's Free Trade Agreement

Chile's Free Trade Agreement	
Nature of the Agreement	Bilateral
Date and Repercussion	Effective January 2004. The agreement represented a milestone in the return to the bilateralism logic of US trade agreements with other countries in the world. The impact of the agreement was seen throughout the commercial world - mainly in the economic blocs.
Breakdown of Multilateralist logic	Yes. There was a break with the Multilateralist logic.
Adoption of the Bilateralism logic	Yes. There was full adoption of the Bilateralist logic.
General Conclusion	The US agreement with Chile represents the first indication of a continuation of bilateral trade logic in American trade strategy. From our analysis, we can conclude that this agreement was of fundamental importance to break, in the international market, the hegemony of the multilateralist model.

Source: Prepared by the Author (2020).

U.S x Korea Free Trade Agreement

The US-Korea Free Trade Agreement entered into force on March 15, 2012. The United States and the Republic of Korea signed the United States-Korea Free Trade Agreement (KORUS FTA) on June 30, 2007. Korea is currently the sixth largest goods trading partner with the US, with a total of $ 130.8 billion (bidirectional) of goods traded by 2018. Below, in table 5, the application of the analysis:

Table 5 - U.S x Korea Free Trade Agreement

U.S x Korea Free Trade Agreement	
Nature of the Agreement	Bilateral
Date and Repercussion	Signed in 2007 and effective from January 2012. The agreement represented a historic moment for a new commercial relationship between the United States and the countries of the Asian continent. The agreement had great repercussions in the international market.
Breakdown of Multilateralist logic	Yes. There was a break with the Multilateralist logic.
Adoption of the Bilateralism logic	Yes. There was full adoption of the Bilateralist logic.
General Conclusion	The US agreement with Korea, although it underwent some changes and came into force well after its signature, represents a milestone in the American bilateralism trade trajectory with Asian countries.

Source: Prepared by the Author (2020).

U.S x COLOMBIA TRADE AGREEMENT

The Trade Promotion Agreement (TPA) between the United States and Colombia entered into force on May 15, 2012. TPA is a comprehensive free trade agreement that provides for the elimination of tariffs and removes barriers to US services, including services and financial resources. The Agreement includes important disciplines on technical barriers to trade, electronic commerce, customs administration and trade facilitation, investments, government procurement, telecommunications, intellectual property rights and environmental and labor protection. Below, in Table 6, the application of the analysis categories:

Table 6 - U.S-Colombia trade agreement

U.S-Colombia trade agreement	
Nature of the Agreement	Bilateral
Date and Repercussion	Signed and effective as of May 15, 2012. This agreement had great relevance in the commercial context of the United States with the countries of Central and Latin America.
Breakdown of Multilateralist logic	Yes. There was a break with the Multilateralist logic.
Adoption of the Bilateralism logic	Yes. There was full adoption of the Bilateralist logic.
General Conclusion	The agreement paved the way for others that would later take place between the United States and the countries of Central and Latin America in isolation. A considerable break in the logic of trade negotiations with these countries, with a great impact, mainly for Colombia.

Source: Prepared by the Author (2020).

U.S x Japan Trade Agreement

On October 7, 2019, the U.S.-Japan Trade Agreement was signed. The US-Japan Digital Trade Agreement was also signed on the same occasion. The US-Japan Trade Agreement eliminated or reduced tariffs on certain agricultural and industrial products to increase bilateral trade in a robust, stable and mutually beneficial manner between nations, which together account for approximately 30% of the global gross domestic monetary influx. Below, in Table 7, the application of the researched categories:

Table 7 - U.S x Japan Trade Agreement

U.S x Japan Trade Agreement	
Nature of the Agreement	Bilateral
Date and Repercussion	Signed and effective as of October 7, 2019. This agreement is the most recent signed by the American Government, under the management of President Donald Trump. The pact was widely passed on to the international market and marked for the first time in decades, a trade agreement between two rich countries.
Breakdown of Multilateralist logic	Yes. There was a break with the Multilateralist logic.
Adoption of the Bilateralism logic	Yes. There was full adoption of the Bilateralist logic.
General Conclusion	The agreement represents a milestone in the resumption of the bilateralism logic of American trade agreements. As we can see, a series of agreements were signed during the 2000s that left the multilateral logic and started to stand out for a commercial relationship between countries in isolation (bilateralism).

Source: Prepared by the Author (2020).

FINAL CONSIDERATIONS

This study dealt with an objective system within a defined methodology, so that facts were analyzed, developed, and documented in such a way that, within the methodological rigidity, the possibility of demonstrating the results that could and were achieved through it was possible.

A scenario of relevant change for the world economic order that was deduced, and now, after the research evidence, it is proven with indications coming from the commercial agreements and signed by the American government over the last 20 years.

The theoretical framework was initiated with the mapping of the concept of possible scenarios for globalization. A reflection that led to consider that this phenomenon had great emphasis from the point of view of dissemination from the Second World War, and ended up dominating the whole world, seeking in one way or another, to alleviate the differences between the countries, giving an opportunity of work for those who were located in countries with less business opportunities, with a more delayed industrialized process, in order to increase their work capacity and obtain more revenue where they could have, in the end, a greater balance between nations.

Globalization, on the other hand, has significantly increased global trade, causing countries to seek and manage lower product costs. Also, offered directly to the public, reducing inflationary processes in each country in some way and increasing the purchasing power and comfort of the general public.

As identified throughout the research, the globalization process has gradually been transformed. On one hand, the globalization of all countries, but on the other, the regions sought to keep this exchange more focused within their own countries, making them the main beneficiaries of this free exchange of products and services. The most typical example of that is Europe, where more than 80% of international trade between the nations that make up the European Union takes place between the countries themselves. This ended up limiting globalization because only the negotiations between two strong blocs could generate business and with that, benefiting mainly their population, but preventing this global trade from taking place in any way without barriers, as blocs dealt with closing its borders to globalization of trade and services as a whole.

This process of globalization, based on the concept of multilateralism that has been studied, ended up in some way being frayed for the various reasons that the world ended up finding. First, there were economic blocs closing their borders and making it difficult for countries from other blocs to enter.

Secondly, based on what was found in the survey, there is a weakening of the WTO itself, which is no longer able to impose stricter rules on the signatory countries. China, as seen, is an example of that.

Thirdly, the regional blocs also began to weaken as they did not serve the group of component countries, resulting in the case like Brexit in which England proposed to leave the bloc as it did not find any advantageous economic sense.

Finally, it is observed that globalization ended up being dominated, from the financial point of view, by the large financial corporations that with much more agility than the provision of other types of services and, mainly, with much more agility than the production and commercialization of products, went ahead and obtained bilateral agreements in the investment area, thus encouraging those bilateral agreements to also be extended to the commercial area.

It is also valid to consider that with regard to this change, the context of the WTO has been changing over the past few years. When it was created two decades ago, many considered that the WTO's proposals regarding economic globalization would be well accepted and would have the natural consequence of successive trade liberalization.

However, trade policy continued to be the target of dispute, since it had significant distributional consequences both nationally and internationally.

Trade liberalization has become more controversial due to the increasing variety of actors finding their place in multilateral trade negotiations and national groups uniting trade with inequality, less prospects and insecurity.

There is no doubt that globalization has made a positive contribution to the world economy. In thirty years, global GDP has jumped from $ 22 trillion to approximately $ 90 trillion. The number of people living in extreme poverty has decreased dramatically and the spread of technology has led to high productivity gains that have been replicated in various areas of the world. And it was also observed that the social losses coming from the globalized world had never been so significant.

After a certain point, it became clear that the globalization processes had reached their limit because the rules in place to manage them did not protect all parties equally. As an example, the level of protection provided to workers in China differed from that provided to workers in Germany, in the United States companies could not compete with prices in other countries, causing damage to the American workers in terms of salary and quality of life.

In this scenario of imbalances, the population began to realize the damage caused by the globalization process, thus emerging a nationalist feeling and a subsequent unwillingness to accept the growth of other nations at the expense of their internal security. Brexit was a great warning about the possibility of an end to globalization, as the departure of the United Kingdom from the largest commercial unit created was an evident symptom that the globalization process is flawed and needs care.

What can be inferred from this research is the possibility that a new globalization is in full structure, precisely from the bilateral agreements that have been carried out, as will be discussed later.

Therefore, in the scenario of productive transformations that are taking place in the world, it is essential to review the form of elaboration of public policies in the productive sector, especially if we consider the need for greater integration with international trade policies. Free trade only works efficiently if the rules can be followed by all countries involved, in order to establish fair globalized trade.

Some countries have formed oligopolies as a result of globalization, making market competition nearly impossible. Due to cheap labor, dumping from non-democratic countries was able to concentrate production of certain products, causing unquantifiable harm to national companies in democratic countries.

In this way, over time, global industries have become increasingly reliant on China's oligopolies. The world's reliance on what the Chinese produce and consume has risen dramatically in the last two decades. However, if China stops, the rest of the world will follow suit.

With the Covid-19 crisis, the company's monopoly on the production of masks and respirators, items in high demand all over the world at this historic time, has gained international attention. An American citizen known as one of the greatest capitalist symbols to this day owns the largest mask factory in China. This shows that the western democratic system is defenseless in the face of the dumping of undemocratic regimes. Entrepreneurs in democratic western countries themselves prefer to invest in China.

Therefore, what is inferred is that more than factories returning to their country of origin, in the coming years, businesses will be seen diversifying the supply chain so that they are no longer as dependent on a single country, such as China, for example. Thus, it is possible that the coronavirus could, in addition to destroying the economy of 2020, radically change the course of history.

The trade war between the United States and China, as discussed in this paper, was already threatening globalization in terms of multilateralism. This created a fierce competition for technology, causing the two countries to drift apart. This decoupling now affects the service sector and the industrial sector in view of the greater risks of acting directly with the Chinese market and relying on information provided by Beijing.

In the face of so many uncertainties and changes, there are also major challenges in relation to the supply chain being able to supply demand quickly and efficiently, which means regionalization and an internalization of production. This is a more resistant model, however, with lower growth.

Enabling the WTO to establish more equality in a scenario where the global trade system is an increasingly confusing system, is paramount to prevent rules and approaches from being conflicted and fragmented. It will be necessary to develop ways of accessing other countries' markets in order to reduce the gap between the most advanced members and those who advance more slowly.

However, it is necessary to pay attention to the growing inequality so that unfair protectionist measures are avoided, guaranteeing the legitimacy of international trade. While it takes time to recognize this trend, many governments have done more to allow citizens to better take advantage of the opportunities of economic globalization, although this is a very difficult task.

In light of the populist unrest seen in some countries, reconciliation must include a reform in the articulation of societal preferences and the definition of trade policy objectives. And, most importantly, fair national distributive policies to complement free trade, limiting its disruptive potential and, therefore, reversing the direction of economic nationalism.

Globalization is the result of decades of work to unify people in their common interest. As a result, even in a more bilateralistic logic, it is necessary and must be preserved through the establishment of new rules that must be followed by all parties involved in order to ensure fair trade.

The globalization process mentioned in this study, showed that the big corporations lost their national identity and started to seek only for their own interests, this may have caused some nations to seek again for the control of the state in relation to the titles of trade practice in such a way as to safeguard the jobs and consumption capacity of its population, which resulted in several bilateral agreements that were gradually being implemented and replacing the then prevailing logic of multilateralism, especially over the last 20 years.

This work aimed to study precisely the American commercial context in this scenario. An in-depth analysis of the commercial agreements signed by the American governments in the last 20 years, that has begun to identify their ideological nature and the commercial impacts arising from this transaction.

This mapping began with previous governments' agreements with Chile and Colombia and progressed to treaties signed by the current Trump administration, which, as the analysis shows, is breaking virtually all multilateral agreements and establishing bilateral or just regional agreements. As was the case in North America or, bilateral such as those in Japan and Korea, in which the interest of each country ended up prevailing over the global idea.

Below, is the general framework of analysis of the agreements that show a chronology of abandoning the multilateralist logic towards bilateralism:

Table 8 - Chronology of abandoning multilateral model towards bilateral

Trade Agreement	Date	Dominant Logic
Trans-Pacific Free Trade Agreement	1994	Multilateralism
North American Free Trade Agreement – NAFTA	1994	Multilateralism
Chile's Free Trade Agreement	2004	Bilateralism
U.S X Korea Free Trade Agreement	2012	Bilateralism
U.S X Colombia trade agreement	2012	Bilateralism
U.S X Japan Trade Agreement	2019	Bilateralism

Source: Prepared by the Author (2020).

This appears to be the trend that has been observed for at least the past four years, and that may or may not continue depending on the next administration that takes over American policy, as a clear distinction is noted between candidate Biden's globalism and the Trump administration's bilateralism.

Regardless, whoever wins the next presidential run, international trade rules should in general, seek a logic less linked to the multilateralist strategy, which, as seen in the micro reasons presented in this study, is in the process of weakening and more interested in the bilateral model that considers the occasional distinctions between the countries.

In general, this presumption can be pursued in the coming years to see what may or may not be the end, but rather the reshaping of the international trade model between countries. A challenge that will impose new standards for the diplomatic corps between countries, as well as a new global political order that takes this current phenomenon into account.

BIBLIOGRAPHY

Abdul-Hak, A.P.N. (2013). The South American defense council: objectives and interests of Brazil. Brasília: FUNAG.

Agnew, J., & Corbridge, S. (1995). Mastering space: hegemony, territory and international political economy. London: Routledge.

Araújo, R. D. (2019). Analysis of the impact of trade agreements: an alternative to traditional models. UNICAMP, Campinas.

Aravena, F. R. (1999). Latin America and international security: contributions and challenges to the 21st century. Washington: Organization of American States.

Badie, B. (2006). What about the XXIe siècle? Le nouveau système international. Paris: La Découverte.

Balassa, B. (1964). Theory of economic integration. Mexico: UTEHA.

Beach, D., & Pedersen, R. B. (2013). Casual case study methods. Michigan: UniPress.

Bhagwati, J. (1999). Regionalism and multilateralism: an overview. In trading blocs: alternative approaches to analyzing preferential trade agreements.Cambridge, MA: MIT Press.

World economic blocs and intergovernmental organizations (figure). Consulted at: mundoeducacao.bol.uol.com.br ,. Accessed on: April 10, 2020.

Bohnenberger, F., & Weinhardt, C. (2017). Malaise in free trade: a new role for the WTO. Nueva Sociedad, (271), 95-109. Consulted at: https://nuso.org/articulo/malestar-en-el-libre-comercio/. Accessed on: 12.Jul.2020.

Carvalho, M., Azevedo, A., & Massuquete, A. (2019). Brazil in the context of the US-China trade war. Porto Alegre: Apencsul.

COMTRADE. (2018). United nations commodity trade statistics, database statistics division. Consulted at: http://comtrade.un.org. Accessed on: 15.jun.2020.

Congress. North American Free Trade Agreement - NAFTA. Consulted at: https://www.congress.gov/bill/103rd-congress/house-bill/3450/text. Accessed on: 26.aug.2020.

Donadelli, L., & Pereira, M. (2019). From multi to bilateralism: history and conjuncture of US foreign and security policies for Latin America. São Paulo: USP.

Enap. (2014). WTO structures and main rules. Consulted at: https://repositorio.enap.gov.br/bitstream/1/3095/3/Estrutura%20e%20Principal%20Regras%20da%20OMC%20%281%29.pdf. Accessed on: 10.apr. 2020.

Evans G., & Menon A. (2017). Brexit and british politics. Cambridge: Wiley.

Farto, M. (2006). Contemporary economic diplomacy. Consulted at: http://janusonline.pt/2006/2006_3_2_1.html. Accessed on: 14.aug.2020.

Fernandes, S., & Simão, L. (2019). Multilateralism: concepts and practices in the 21st century. Coimbra: Press.Gama, C. F. P. S. (2020). The UK leaves the European Union in a partially globalized world in crisis. Conjuncture Bulletin (BOCA), 1 (2), 28-31.

Gama, C. F. P. S., & Camargo, F. F. (2018). From Farmers to Firms: United States and China in a Shifting World Order. International situation, 15 (2), 11-21.

Gonçalves, R. (1999). Globalization and Denationalization. Rio de Janeiro: Peace and Earth.

Huntington, S. P. (1975). Transnational organizations in world politics. Public administration Magazine, 9 (2), 9-45.

Jain, S. C. (2006). Emerging economies and the transformation of international business: Brazil, Russia, India and China (BRICs). Connecticut: Edward Elgar Publishing.

Keohane, R. O. (2002). Power and governance in a partially globalized world. London: Psychology Press.

Kissinger, H. (2012). Diplomacy. São Paulo: Saraiva.

Lafer, C. (1996). The World Trade Organization's dispute settlement system. São Paulo: USP.

Li, N. (2002). China's Foreign Policy Agenda and the PLA's New Mission. RSIS Working Papers. Consulted at: http: // www. rsis. edu. sg / rsis-publication / rsis / 528-chinas-foreign-policy-agend / #. VbKuF_lViko. Accessed on: 01.set.2018.

Magalhães, J. C. (1996). Pure Diplomacy (2nd ed). New Sale: Bertrand.

Ministry of Foreign Affairs. World trade organization. Consulted at: http://www.itamaraty.gov.br/pt-BR/politica-externa/diplomacia-economica-comercial-e-financeira/132-organizacao-mundial-do-comercio-omc. Accessed on: April 13, 2020.

Ministry of Commerce of the People's Republic of China MOFCOM. (2018). Announcement on imposing tariffs on some goods originating in the US. Consulted at: http://english.mofcom.gov.cn/article/newsrelease/significantnews/201806/20180602757681.shtml. Accessed on: 25.mar.2020.

Ministry of Development, Industry and Foreign Trade MDIC (2018). Accumulated Brazilian trade balance for the year 2017. Consulted at: https://www.mdic.gov.br/index.php/comercio-exterior/estatisticas-de-comercio-exterior/balancacomercial-brasileira-acumulado-do-ano?layout = edit & id = 3056. Accessed on: February 2.2020.

Niblett, R .; & Bhardwaj, G. (2019). Why we build walls: 30 years after the fall of the Berlin Wall. Chatham House. Consulted at: https://www.chathamhouse.org/expert/comment/why-we-build-walls-30-years-after-fall-berlin-wall   ?. Accessed on: April 10, 2020.

Petri, F., & Weber, B. (2006). The effects of globalization on the integration of economic blocs. Santa Maria: UFSM.

Pinto, P. C. A. (2015). Diplomacy and defense policy: Brazil in the debate on hemispheric security in the post-Cold War decade (1990-2000). Brasília: FUNAG.

Plihon, D. (2007). Financial globalization. Coimbra: Unicoimbra.

Pontes, J. N. M. O. (2016). Portuguese foreign policy: bilateralism and multilateralism. Revista Lusíada, 13 (14), 71-112. Consulted at: http://revistas. lis.ulusiada.pt/index.php/lpis/article/view/2434. Accessed on: 2.ago.2020.

PRADO, Luiz Carlos Delorme. Globalization: notes on a controversial concept. Available at <https://dogmaseenigmas.files.wordpress.com/2012/12/ prado-2000.pdf>. Accessed on July 12, 2020.

Ramos, L., Vadell J., Saggioro A., & Fernandes A. (2012). Global economic governance and the challenges of the G20 after the financial crisis: analysis of the positions of the USA, China, Germany and Brazil. Brazilian Journal of International Politics, 55 (2). Consulted at: https://www.scielo.br/scielo. php?pid=S0034-73292012000200002&script=sci_arttext&tlng=pt. Accessed on: 12.Jun.2020.

Rebel Tecnologia and Banking Correspondent. (2018). Understand what financial globalization is and how it works. Consulted at: https://blog.rebel. com.br/entenda-o-que-e-a-globalizacao-financeira-e-como-ela-funciona/. Accessed on: 30.mar.2020.

Seawrigth, J., & Gerring, J. Case selection techniques in case study research: a menu of qualitative and quantitative options. Consulted at: https://journals. sagepub.com/doi/10.1177/1065912907313077 / Accessed at: 12.jul.2020.

Sennes, R. (2003). Changes in foreign policy in the 1980s: a newly industrialized middle power. Porto Alegre: UFRGS Publisher.

Silva, D. C. A., & Loureiro, H. A. C. (2009). Efforts and Reinforcements: composition of national responses to the 2008 crisis in the USA and Germany. Electronic Journal of Social Sciences, 3 (8), 127-149. Consulted at: http:// periodicos.ufjr.br/index.php/csonline/article/view/17127. Accessed on: 21.ago.2020.

Souto, C. (2005). Bilateralism and multilateralism before and after nationalism ends. Consulted at: http://cdn.fee.tche.br/jornadas/2/H2-05.pdf. Accessed on: 13.jul.2020.

Souza, J. L. (2008). Integration: regionalization in globalization. Ipea Magazine. Consulted at: https://www.ipea.gov.br/desafios/index.php?option=com_content&view=article&id=1178:reportagens-materias&Itemid=39, Accessed at: 13.apr.2020.

Stiglitz, J. E. (2002). Globalization: the great disappointment. Lisbon: Terramar.

Teixeira, C. G. P. (2014). A policy for the continent: reinterpreting the Monroe doctrine. Brazilian Journal of International Politics, 57 (2), p.115-132.

European Union. Regulation (Eu) No. 1219/2012 of the European Parliament and the Council. Consulted at: http://eurlex.europa.eu/LexUriServ/LexUriServ.do?uri=OJ:L:2012:351:0040:0046:PT:PDF. Accessed on: June 20, 2016.

USTR. (2018). Office of the United States trade representative. Consulted at: https://ustr.gov/abouts/policy-offices/press-office/press-releases/2018/jun/ustr-issues-tariffs-chinese-products. Accessed on: 30.jul.2020.

USTR. US-Colombia trade agreement. Consulted at: https://ustr.gov/trade-agreements/free-trade-agreements/colombia-tpa. Accessed on: 26.aug.2020.

USTR. USA vs. Japan Trade Agreement. Consulted at: https://ustr.gov/countries-regions/japan-korea-apec/japan/us-japan-trade-agreement-negotiations/us-japan-trade-agreement-text. Accessed on: 26.aug.2020.

USTR. Chile's free trade agreement. Consulted at: https://ustr.gov/trade-agreements/free-trade-agreements/chile-fta. Accessed on: 26.aug.2020.

USTR. USA v Korea free trade agreement. Consulted at: https://ustr.gov/trade-agreements/free-trade-agreements/korus-fta. Accessed on: 26.aug.2020.

USTR. Trans-Pacific Free Trade Agreement. Consulted at: https://ustr.gov/trade-agreements/free-trade-agreements/trans-pacific-partnership/tpp-full-text. Accessed on: 26.aug.2020.

Vitelli, M. G. (2018). Cooperative Security. In: Saint-Pierre, H. L. (org). Dictionary of security and defense (194). São Paulo: Unesp Digital.

Wei, D. (2010). Bilateral investment promotion and protection agreements: practices in Brazil and China. Nation and Defense, 125 (4), 157-191. Consulted at: https://core.ac.uk/download/pdf/62688837.pdf. Accessed on: 01.may.2020.

World Trade Organization (figure 1). Consulted at: https://www.wto.org/. Accessed on: April 13, 2020.

www.ingramcontent.com/pod-product-compliance
Lightning Source LLC
Chambersburg PA
CBHW071457210326
41597CB00018B/2580